THE FIRST HUNDRED YEARS

*From
horse carriages —
to automobiles —
to jet planes*

THE FIRST HUNDRED YEARS
by Florence Parker Simister

Rhode Island Hospital Trust Company, Providence, Rhode Island   1967

1.16.68

CONTENTS

Foreword 7

Backward in Time 9

Chapter One, 1867-1876 14

Chapter Two, 1877-1886 26

Chapter Three, 1887-1896 38

Chapter Four, 1897-1906 50

Chapter Five, 1907-1916 62

Chapter Six, 1917-1926 74

Chapter Seven, 1927-1936 90

Chapter Eight, 1937-1946 106

Chapter Nine, 1947-1956 116

Chapter Ten, 1957-1966 128

Forward in Time 142

Board of Directors 144

Staff 145

Acknowledgments 153

Clarence H. Gifford, Jr.
President and Chief Executive Officer

FOREWORD

To the general public a bank's one hundredth anniversary may be only of passing interest, but to its customers, stockholders, directors, officers, and employees it is a significant milestone. The Rhode Island Hospital Trust Company has published this book of its "first hundred years" knowing that a number of people will find it interesting, not only as a history of Hospital Trust, but also as a documentary of the era during which the Bank has grown and prospered.

We hope this book will find a permanent place in your home or office. We are sending copies to schools and libraries as another addition to the valuable historical data already available.

"It's been a colorful century" is the slogan for our centennial observance, and surely it has been colorful.

Just think of the many changes that have come about during this period. In transportation we have gone from steamboats and steam trains to atomic-powered ships and electric trains, from horse carriages to automobiles, from the balloon to the airplane to jets to rockets. And in communication we have seen the development of the telegraph, telephone, wireless, radio, and television. Indeed, in science, theology, and medicine the forward steps have been miraculous while many other changes have made life more secure, more enjoyable, and more worthwhile.

In banking we have seen the growth of a wide network of branch offices to make it easier to do business with us, and today the computer is making possible better service and additional services.

As we pause to observe this passing "colorful century" we are at the same time aware that the future can be even brighter. It will be the responsibility of all of us at Hospital Trust to make it so.

Clarence H. Gifford, Jr., *President*

7

First Rhode Island Regiment on parade before departing for Washington — 1861

BACKWARD IN TIME

In 1867 the events of the Civil War, while not remote, were becoming blurred in retrospect. The gaps in family groups caused by the loss of husbands, brothers, fathers, and sons had not been closed, but people had learned to live with their grief.

The consequences of the war, however, were still apparent. The newspapers carried reminders to discharged soldiers that bounties would be paid them; some men were writing memoirs of the campaigns; many states were trying to collect claims against the government for expenses incurred during the rebellion.

Andrew Johnson was President, but the search for the men involved in the assassination of Abraham Lincoln went on. It was almost two years since that crime had been committed and John Surratt, one of the last suspects to be apprehended, was about to be brought to trial.

In spite of the widespread horror at the murder of the President there was a general lessening of tension, a release from the excitement and dread of the previous years. It was, in fact, a time of material progress and prosperity. The climate was mild and sunny in 1867, the ground fertile. The seeds sown that year, sprouted, took root, and grew. The time was right.

A summary of the preceding year showed that four and one-half million dollars had been spent in construction throughout Rhode Island. The buildings (some not yet finished) included homes, stores, schools, and a general hospital in Providence. Street railways had come to Rhode Island in 1863 and these stimulated both the urban and suburban communities. People left the slums in the city and found decent housing within reach of the railways. In addition to these suburban developments there were the villages clustered around the mills which had sprung up along most of the rivers of the state. Now all the wealth accumulated by the merchant-seamen of the eighteenth century was being poured into these manufacturing villages. People again had the time to think of peaceful matters, of technical advances in industry, of charitable works, of the establishment of a new bank.

On the first day of January, 1867, the *Providence Daily Journal* carried an editorial which began: "We have actually passed into a new period of time, numbered 1867 . . . The earth gets through its revolutions and comes full circle in 365 days, but few things in human life stick so close to the almanac. And yet the year is a manageable period, to look forward to, to look back upon. It contains events enough, the result of what began long ago, the beginning of what is to be completed in some years to come, for us to bring them under inspection and give them date."

One of the events of that year "that should be given date" occurred at the May session of the Rhode Island General Assembly meeting at Newport. On Wednesday, May 30, 1867, there was a listing in the *Evening Bulletin:* "Petition of Rhode Island Hospital Trust Company (from the House) was referred to the committee on corporations, reported back and accompanying act passed in concurrence." This item was followed by another under news of the House of Representatives: "An act to incorporate the Rhode Island Hospital Trust Company was read and passed."

The germ of this idea had been planted four years earlier when another charter was granted by the General Assembly, this one for a hospital in Providence. "After the granting of the act of incorporation the citizens of the state and city were invited to subscribe the necessary funds to build the hospital." Captain Thomas Poynton Ives, a medical student and the Hospital's first benefactor, pledged $10,000. He died in France in 1865 at the age of thirty-one, and in his will he left $50,000 more to the Hospital. He had earlier induced his father, Moses Brown Ives, to leave a bequest of $40,000 to a hospital in Providence when one should be built. Moses Brown Ives died in 1857.

One of the concerns of the Board of Trustees of the new hospital was to insure the continued support of their organization. The public was generous with subscriptions during the war, but it was felt that these would drop off at the end of hostilities and continued support through the years ahead had to be found. They, therefore, decided to form a trust company, with the money on hand, to furnish the assistance required.

Trust companies were a new development in banking in the nineteenth century, the first one having been founded in 1822 in New York. "They combined," one source says, "the functions of savings banks with the functions of banks of discounts and demand deposits. They have had in Rhode

Rhode Island Hospital
Chartered 1863, Opened in 1868

Washington Row 1843-1916
Site of present Head Office

Island a development paralleled by that in no other state. They were free from the taxes on deposits and capital which were imposed on the national banks. Their beginning was opportune because it coincided with the period of Reconstruction."

For many months prior to May 29, 1867, the day the charter was granted to the Rhode Island Hospital Trust Company, many of the most influential and philanthropic-minded gentlemen of Providence had been discussing with the trustees of the Hospital the idea of petitioning the General Assembly for an enabling instrument. Preston H. Gardner, who was associated with the Trust Company for sixty-nine years, once wrote: "It [the Bank] owed its existence to the desire of a few public-spirited men to create what should be a financial institution of high credit and powerful resources and, at the same time, prove a pecuniary helper to the Rhode Island Hospital, a benevolent institution then in its infancy."

Robert H. Ives, uncle of Captain Thomas Poynton Ives and brother of Moses Brown Ives, who was active in founding the Hospital (he donated $25,000) and the Bank, wrote a letter early in 1867 to the Actuary of the Massachusetts Hospital Life Insurance Company inquiring as to whether the company's profit-sharing arrangement with the Massachusetts General Hospital had proven harmful to the company and its trust depositors. The answer from the Actuary was enlightening. He said: "In reply to your question whether this provision is upon the whole a pecuniary detriment to the Institution, I answer that it is not. . . . Upon the whole I should say that if I were seeking the establishment of an institution for the same general purposes, which this now accomplishes, I should as a matter of policy, advise the insertion of some similar provision in favor of some great unequivocal public charity."

Because it was hoped that the Rhode Island Hospital Trust Company would be a financial aid to the Rhode Island Hospital, its charter was unique in its day being the first "upon which was imposed in lieu of a tax the obligation to devote a certain portion of its profits to charitable purposes. The Company was required to pay one-third of its net income over 6 per cent to the Rhode Island Hospital as long as the legislature should grant no similar charter to parties other than its incorporators."

The name of the new trust company followed from the name of the still-unopened hospital and from the function this trust company would perform for that institution: it would furnish the financial support required.

On October 24, 1867, the first meeting of the Rhode Island Hospital Trust Company was called to elect officers of the Company. The meeting was

Early view of Westminster Street looking east from Green Street

held at the Providence Horse Guards' Armory at 11 Westminster Street. The command had leased the rooms formerly known as Westminster Hall, had redecorated them, and announced that they were to be used for lectures and concerts as well as drills and as a "central location for meetings of merchants and as a business exchange." The choice of that place, although perhaps not made with intent, was significant. The Horse Guards had been founded in 1842 and one of the charter members had been Moses Brown Ives, who had left a bequest to a hospital in Providence when one should be built. Oddly enough, this corps had been detailed for special guard duty at the United States General Hospital at Portsmouth Grove, Portsmouth, Rhode Island, and at the Providence Marine Hospital then located where the Rhode Island Hospital was to stand.

In 1966 the stockholders still meet in the same geographical location as did the incorporators in 1867. The Sabin Block, numbered 7, 9, 11, 13, and 15 Westminster Street, where the Providence Horse Guards rented rooms, was purchased by the Rhode Island Hospital Trust Company in 1890. It was razed and the Hospital Trust Building was erected on the site. Four of the street numbers were then discarded, but number 15 was retained as the Bank's permanent address. It is still the street number of the Head Office of the Rhode Island Hospital Trust Company in Providence, the oldest trust company in New England.

13

CHAPTER ONE

Upper Providence Harbor — 1867

1867-1876

On July 5, 1867, the following letter was received by some prominent men in Providence:

Dear Sir:

  I am requested on behalf of corporators of the Rhode Island Hospital Trust Company to call a meeting for purposes of organization at the office of R. H. Ives, Esq., South Main Street, for Wednesday, July 10, 3 P.M.

The letter was signed by William Binney, a lawyer in Providence who was on the Auditing Committee for the Rhode Island Hospital, a member of its Executive Committee, and one of the group of men who had been discussing the possibility of founding a trust company. He is sometimes called the organizer of the Rhode Island Hospital Trust Company, and he was probably the man to suggest the obvious name of the Company which was already being used in this first communication.

  Three months later another letter went out requesting the recipients to meet a few of the subscribers to the Rhode Island Hospital Trust Company at Brown & Ives Counting House, Friday, October 11. Less than a fortnight later, on October 24, a meeting was held at the Providence Horse Guards' Armory to elect a Board of Directors, a President, and a Secretary. The first Board numbered seventeen men and included all but two of the original incorporators. William Binney, the moving spirit of the enterprise, was elected President, and he gave up his law practice so that he could devote his time to the Trust Company. Christopher Lippitt was elected temporary Secretary. During the following months the Directors met in the office of the President, in the Blackstone Block, 27-33 Weybosset Street.

  The new company's name was its first advertisement; it was a bid for favor from a public to which trust companies were unknown. It reflected the benefit the charitable institution (Rhode Island Hospital) would receive from

William Binney
President 1867-1881

the new business enterprise (Rhode Island Hospital Trust Company). Another reason for the name, we are told, is that "it was the first trust company to be established in New England. Because of the unfamiliarity among the people of the state with what was proposed, it needed a favorable introduction to the public and to the General Assembly from which the charter was sought." People were aware of state banks and of national banks which did banking by means of circulation based on government securities, but the business of trust companies was confined to banking by means of deposits. Mr. Binney inspected a trust company in Philadelphia and one in New York but felt that wider scope was wanted in Providence. The Bank was, therefore, empowered by its charter to "receive money in trust or on deposit and to act as Administrator, Assignee, or Receiver whether by appointment of Court or of Individuals."

At the first meeting of the Board of Directors on Tuesday, December 3, 1867, at Mr. Binney's office, eleven men were present. Their names were entered in the minutes as Mr. Binney, Alfred Anthony, A. C. Barstow, Z. Chafee, Robert H. Ives, Edward King, Christopher Lippitt, Earl P. Mason, Samuel M. Noyes, Edward D. Pearce, and Amos D. Smith. One of the items on the agenda of "Subjects for Deliberation" was "the location of the Company's place of business and the expenses of the officers of the Company." It was decided to find a suitable place "not higher than the second floor with two rooms if practicable and to procure the necessary safe and office furniture." A corporate seal was also decided on with the words "Rhode Island Hospital Trust Company" printed around the rim and "Incorporated A.D. 1867" in the center. A committee was appointed to open Books of Subscription to complete the capital stock to the sum of $500,000. The Books were to be closed the last day of February, 1868. That first Board of Directors also had the job of designating some bank where "all the moneys received by the Company were to be deposited daily." The Blackstone Canal National Bank was chosen. Rooms were finally rented on the second floor of the Mechanics Bank Building at 37 South Main Street.

There is in existence a memorandum: "Orders for filling Company rooms by Christopher Lippitt with instructions to carry it out." The note lists what was to be done to the rooms on South Main Street and how they were to be furnished:

Painting of walls to approach dull light buff color and panelled
Railing across the room to separate inner office from the outer this to be replaced with
    a kind of counter if after occupying the rooms it shall be deemed preferable — or a

more solid division than railing may now be set up
Standing desk about 12 feet long with platform
Sitting desk with flat top and drawers to floor covered with billiard cloth or enameled
    cloth of large size
Two good heavy chairs on swivels
Office chairs
Table for Directors' room
Chairs for Directors' room
Brussels carpet for inside of railing and Directors' room
Heavy oil cloth outside of railing
Stoves with open grates
Sign adopted to the space alloted for it

      There is also extant a sheet of paper with the words on it "Plan for recording trusts — November 11, 1867. Sample of Daily Tickler — January 1, 1868." This projection of the first day of the year is one of the few pieces of written evidence that the Bank hoped to open on January 1. Most sources say that it opened some time in January, 1868, but Herbert J. Wells, President of the Bank from 1884 to 1919, in one of his reports refers to January 1 as the opening date, and in the State Bank Commissioner's report for 1909 the Rhode Island Hospital Trust Company is listed with a notation: "Incorporated May, 1867. Commenced business January 1, 1868."

      On April 2, 1868, the first deposit was made by Samuel Powel of Newport, Mr. Binney's son-in-law. On May 7 the signature of Samuel A. Parker was sent to the Bank for the Signature Book. He was the General Treasurer of Rhode Island and on May 15 the Company could insert this notice in the *Providence Daily Evening Press:* "Rhode Island Hospital Trust Company. We invite the attention of our readers to the advertisement in another column of the above-named company as a depository for investments while the fact that it has been selected as the fiscal agent of the State will give it a high place among our many good and safe institutions of deposit and trust." The next day in the *Providence Daily Herald* the advertisement stated: "The Rhode Island Hospital Trust Company is the financial agent of the State of Rhode Island and also the city of Providence." At the meeting of the Board of Directors on May 12, 1868, the subject of advertising had been discussed. The President had suggested the form of the advertisements; they had been read and approved. Also approved were the suggestions that copies of the charter be printed and that the purposes of the Company be issued in pamphlet form. Mr. Binney had then signed an agreement with Charles Wheeler, who owned a newspaper advertising agency, "to insert advertising for the Trust Company

... to be in *Providence Press, Providence Herald, Newport Mercury, Bristol Phenix, Woonsocket Patriot, Narragansett Weekly*, one copy of each paper to come by mail."

The first mortgage oddly enough was on property at the corner of Hospital and Lockwood Streets. The first loan was made on March 31. The first rent was paid to the Mechanics Bank in July. The first investment was made on January 15, 1868. The first trust account came to the Bank on July 6, 1868, under the will of William E. Greene, the Bank being named trustee. This account terminated in 1915 when the last beneficiary died. The first balance sheet, dated May 30, 1868, showed that $352,500 of the authorized capital stock of $500,000 had been paid in and that deposits of slightly over $40,000 had been received.

By October, 1869, there were 170 depositors with accounts subject to check at sight and the Finance Committee reported that it "allows an interest

Early view of Broad Street (now Weybosset) about 1871 — City Hotel in center of picture

Soldiers and Sailors Monument 1871 — in its first location at west end of Exchange Place

on the daily balance at the rate of four per cent per annum and that interest is made up and credited on active accounts monthly, on others at the end of six months." It also reported that it received "moneys in any amount on deposit accounts subject to check on sight" to differentiate between these and participation accounts. There were seventy-four of the latter kind by the fall of 1869, and for several years the participation deposits amounted to more than the checking deposits. Until 1917 the initial deposit required in a participation account was $500. In 1917, $100 became the minimum deposit required. In 1928 this was reduced to $1.00, and the name "participation" was changed to "savings." A report on the trust accounts, dated October, 1869, showed that the amount held in trust was $388,519.69.

The Bank was growing because of the assiduous work of the President and the other officers and because the state was growing. In 1871 Smithfield was divided into three towns: Smithfield, North Smithfield, and Lincoln. Two years later a portion of Cranston was annexed to Providence and formed into Roger Williams Park. In 1874 North Providence was divided in three, one part given to Providence, one to Pawtucket, and one remaining North Providence. The city of Providence itself was spreading out in all directions necessitating new bridges, new roads, and better transportation.

The men of the Rhode Island Hospital Trust Company were keenly aware of the burgeoning community outside their doors and of their dependence on it and their duty to it. Mr. Binney, the President, stated that the design of the Bank was originally "to conduct all its business with reference primarily to the financial interests of the community, then of its depositors of all kinds, then of its stockholders." Mr. Binney took a leading role in community affairs. He was president of the Common Council of Providence, a member of the Rhode Island General Assembly, and author of the City Charter for Providence which had been accepted by the General Assembly in 1866. Another outside interest of his is revealed in the minutes of the Directors' meeting of September, 1872. They note that when the meeting was called to order "the President was unavoidably absent being chairman of the city committee appointed to test the Point Street Bridge."

The growth of the Company took many forms. One was the solidifying of relations with the Rhode Island Hospital which had finally opened its doors on October 1, 1868. To this end a committee of two, Moses B. Lockwood and William Binney, was appointed by the Bank in 1871 to meet with a similar committee from the Hospital to review the relations of the two organizations. These men were asked to study the reports of any committees which had been made up to that time on the association of the two corporations and to state what relations had developed and which of these should be continued in the future to serve the best interests of the Hospital and the Trust Company.

Another form of growth was physical. In the fifth year following the granting of the charter, the Rhode Island Hospital Trust Company needed larger quarters, and in 1872 it was decided to purchase the house of Dr. Joseph Mauran at the corner of South Main and Hopkins Streets. Discussion continued into the following spring on the merits of two courses: remodeling the Mauran house or razing it and erecting a new building. In March, 1873, the decision was made to renovate.

The years from 1860 to 1873 were considered a period of great prosperity. Paper money had depreciated to fifty cents on the dollar, but the day of reckoning (when debts would become due in gold valuation) was so long coming that people ceased to be afraid of it. It was so easy to borrow money that there was a temptation to enlarge businesses beyond what was safe.

In the fall of 1873 the day of reckoning came. After a series of catastrophes — a flood in China; ship, train, and mine disasters; an insurrection in Santo Domingo; a Canadian railway scandal — a financial panic developed in New York. In September Jay Cooke and Company, the private banking house in Philadelphia, was forced to suspend and stocks tumbled 3 to 10 per cent. There were runs on banks in Chicago and elsewhere. The stock exchange in New York closed. A Providence newspaper stated: "There has been too much haste and in cities too much recklessness. Too much money has been put where it cannot be recovered and where it pays no interest. . . . This panic will most likely soon be over, the losses have not touched save indirectly the great industries of the country." In October the disturbance was referred to as "The Monetary Convulsion," and financial experts warned that currency was scarce and immediate relief would be obtained if banks and individuals would cease hoarding. Local newspapers blamed the panic on railroad speculation and Wall Street manipulation of the currency and reported that the banks in Providence acted "with liberality and yet with caution and have maintained their own position while affording the necessary assistance to their customers."

Then in November came a great blow. The A. & W. Sprague Manufacturing Company suspended business. This great house had expanded in the easy times of 1860 to 1873 and was using at the time of its failure millions of dollars of borrowed money to engage in a great variety and number of businesses that together formed an empire. The family owned nine mammoth mills in the state and an old saying was that if you saw smoke in Rhode Island, it belonged to the Spragues. The creditors of this large company met in the Horse Guards' Armory with a committee composed of Royal C. Taft and Stephen Harris, of the Rhode Island Hospital Trust Company, and James Y. Smith, former mayor of Providence, to inquire into the condition of the concern. On October 30 there was a meeting of the representatives of the banks "to consider some plan of protection for the depositors" of what were known as Sprague banks: First National, Second National, Globe National, and also, to a lesser extent, the Franklin Savings Bank and the Cranston Savings

Point Street Bridge, built in 1872

Bank. A committee was appointed to hold and administer the property in behalf of the creditors until the obligations were paid.

The business of the A. & W. Sprague Manufacturing Company had increased enormously during the Civil War and in the early seventies their mills printed 1,400,000 yards of calico a week. Now they owed about $7,000,000 but a newspaper reported that "while it is right to take up proper means to prevent such a catastrophe [the failure], it is not right to question the general commercial credit of the community or to frighten people into the belief that the business of Providence and of Rhode Island was to be fatally crippled because one great house expands itself into disaster ... The wealth and enterprise of Rhode Island are not bound up in any one house, nor is its industry dependent on any one employer." This statement can be refuted because the historical fact is that "the industrial supremacy which Rhode Island retained until 1870 was dissipated by the panic of 1873," and the amount of money involved in the Sprague failure "astounded the whole country." It had no parallel in the industrial history of the United States. Rhode Island suffered a blow which had a lasting effect on her industry, and one historian tells us that "scarcely a bank in the state escaped serious losses. The whole period was one of noteworthy industrial depression."

As a result of the Sprague failure national banks consolidated, became trust companies, or were absorbed by trust companies. At least fifteen banks in the state failed, suspended, or reorganized.

In this financial climate, at the Annual Meeting of the Rhode Island Hospital Trust Company on December 3, 1873, a resolution was passed:

Whereas this Company was established mainly with the view of furnishing to the people of this state an institution with every guarantee for fidelity and security ... and whereas the experience of the last three months has demonstrated many dangers to which all such financial institutions have been exposed it is resolved that a special committee of three be appointed to examine and consider the business of this Company as it has been and is now conducted and to report to the Board of Directors any changes in the system of management which they may recommend whereby such dangers may be avoided by this institution and the more perfect security of the Company as a trust company be insured.

A board of inspection was named and also a committee to prepare a bond for each officer and employee of the Company.

On June 1, 1874, in the sixth year of business and the seventh year since incorporation, the Rhode Island Hospital Trust Company started operations at 60 South Main Street. The day the new banking rooms were opened the Bank's total balance (capital and undivided profits) was $691,500 and deposits $5,380,000. The Bank's building was described as "commodious and elegant" by the *Providence Daily Journal*. "All in all," the newspaper account went on, "the new banking rooms of the Rhode Island Hospital Trust Company are worthy of a visit for the gratification of the love of the beautiful and a credit to the judgement and taste of those in charge of the arrangement . . . For light in the nighttime if necessary green bronze gas chandeliers of beautiful design hang over the various desks at the counter each having an argand burner in the centre directly over the desk." In a few years, about 1879, there was to be a telephone on the wall. The calls were few, though, and the person who was needed on the telephone walked to the wall where the instrument was fixed. The Bank's own vaults were in a fireproof addition in the rear of the building, and before they were completed a memorandum was written by one of the officers of the Bank. He did not sign his name to it, but it is filed with old deeds and valuable historical papers. It reads: "One of the covering stones of the top of the vault of the Rhode Island Hospital Trust Company in the addition now being built to the Mauran Building on Hopkins Street is not dowelled . . . so that it may be lifted off if necessary. This stone is the fourth stone from the east and the sixth stone from the west end, there being nine covering stones in all." These vaults still exist, as does the building. It is the home of the Title Guarantee Company of Rhode Island and is now number 66 South Main Street.

Part of the furnishings carried across to the new banking rooms was the first Signature Book, which is still in existence. In it were pasted slips of paper bearing the signatures of depositors and those authorized to do business with the Bank. This was before the day of printed forms and the notes were extremely informal. "Gents," says one dated 1870, "Until otherwise instructed, please pay from funds deposited in your bank to our credit upon checks signed ———— ." And another, written in 1872, reads: "Mr. William Binney, Esquire. Please pay any checks which may be drawn against my account signed by my wife ———— ."

The officers of the Company were concerned about the security of these vaults and a committee was appointed "to invite a meeting of presidents of the banks of the city" and the superintendent of the Holmes Burglar Alarm Telegraph Company for an explanation of the alarm system and a discussion of whether it should be adopted by all the banks in the city or any of them in connection with Hospital Trust.

In 1875 the first of the original corporators died — Robert H. Ives, a member of the Board of Directors. His loss was to be felt keenly, but there were enough men of sagacity left to establish the Company more and more firmly on its foundations.

The foremost of these was the President, William Binney. He was "universally recognized as a man of high efficiency and character." It was said that "He came of a race of scholars and men of affairs and the habit of thinking broadly was always a natural one with him ... The civic sense was at all times strong in him and he found it a keen pleasure ... to be able to render a signal service to the community."

It is this ideal, established by Mr. Binney, the first President of the Rhode Island Hospital Trust Company, that has pervaded the life of this Company and has made it a tower of strength to the community.

Broad Street (now Weybosset) looking west from Mathewson — 1872

CHAPTER TWO

Early photo of City Hall — 1878

1877-1886

The decade beginning with the year 1877 opened inauspiciously. On the world scene Russia and Turkey were about to declare war. Locally a season of lectures was at hand and a talk was given May 8 in the Music Hall on "the marvel of the age, the speaking telephone," the lecturer, Professor A. Graham Bell. The newspaper reported the next day on "the wonderful telephone" and "how it talked and sang."

There was a fair amount of building going on in Providence that year. The roof was put on the new City Hall; the exterior of the Court House and the interior of the Narragansett Hotel were completed; construction was begun on the Brown University Library; two schools (Doyle Avenue and Candace Street) were erected, as well as several business blocks. The harbor facilities in Narragansett Bay and its estuaries were being improved. The channels of the bay and of the Providence and Pawtucket rivers were being widened and dredged. Newport Harbor, too, was being deepened and work on the Block Island breakwater and harbor was begun. This would result, it was hoped, in increased commercial enterprise on the part of Rhode Island manufacturers.

In June President Rutherford B. Hayes came to Rhode Island. He was escorted through long avenues of bunting, and the procession moved along Washington Row and up Westminster Street, two streets that were to become important in the Bank's history. That was also the month when Mr. Binney, who was ill, asked the Board of Directors for a year's leave of absence. His request was granted, but his withdrawal was a source of worry to all. It was to be a year and one-half before he returned to resume his duties.

At the meeting of the Board of Directors the month after Mr. Binney's request was granted it was voted "That the office of Vice President of the Corporation be and is hereby created to terminate July 1, 1878." A committee was appointed to call on Alexander Farnum to "ascertain if he would accept

the office of Vice President of this Company." He agreed and on July 13, 1877, was elected for a year.

Business prospects were poor in 1877 and the prophets said they would not improve until there was a better currency. (This was the time of soft-money parties and hard-money parties, of greenbacks and national bank notes, and of the law, passed in February, 1878, authorizing the coinage of silver dollars.)

In spite of the gloom, the newspapers during the following summer of 1878 were crowded with advertisements for recreation places called summer gardens. Providence had two famous ones: the Park Garden and the San Souci Garden. Excursions to Mount Hope, Block Island, and Narragansett were also advertised. There was horse racing at Narragansett Trotting Park in Cranston, and the Providence baseball club, the Grays, was much in the news. They won the National League Pennant the next summer and in 1884 also flew the world champion flag at their baseball grounds on Messer Street.

By 1878 there was a new County Court House which had been built to replace the old Town House. The Rhode Island School of Design opened in 1878 in a room in the Hoppin Homestead Building, and the Providence Public Library also opened that year in a room in the Butler Exchange, one of the new buildings in downtown Providence.

The office of Vice President was continued from July, 1878, to December of the same year and then to December, 1879, Mr. Farnum being elected Vice President each time. Then, at the Annual Meeting in 1879 a suggestion was made that the office of Vice President be created because "Mr. Binney cannot bear the strain of the same amount and kind of labor rendered previous to his recent absence." However, it was decided not to change the by-laws ("The officers of this corporation . . . shall consist of a President, twenty Directors . . . and such other officers as the Board of Directors shall from time to time appoint") but to "elect from time to time as circumstances may demand someone to fill the position contemplated." This office, in the early years of the Bank's history, was created just that way, at moments of crisis and only when it was voted to create it and to elect someone to fill it. In December, 1879, Mr. Farnum was once more elected Vice President ("in the absence of the President, he shall be clothed with and exercise the same powers of office as belong to the President").

At this same meeting in 1879 the question arose of declaring a special dividend suggested by the stockholders out of a fund known as Commissions: fees paid the Company for its service in management of business as trustee, executor, agent, etc. The President was authorized to secure the opinion of counsel "as to what claim if any the Rhode Island Hospital would have upon this Company by reason of the Board declaring said dividend in case the same should be declared." The advice of counsel was necessary since the Trust Company had agreed to pay to the Hospital one-third of its net income over 6 per cent. The dividend was to be payable after January 20, 1880. Meanwhile the Finance Committee gave long consideration to increasing the capital stock of the Company and to the subject of how much of the surplus earnings of the Company "should be divided out in the form of new stock." In September, 1880, the Rhode Island General Assembly, upon application of the Trust Company, "passed an act in amendment of the charter of this Corporation allowing an increase of its capital to a sum not exceeding one million dollars." The questions of the increase in capital, of creating new stock, and of the amendment of the charter, "all large ones, assumed graver proportions," one source tells us, "in view of the fact that by our [the Bank's] written agreement with the Hospital, that Corporation owns one third of all our surplus earnings whatever the amount may now be, or at any future time may be determined to be." The Finance Committee, therefore, recommended that "if any stock dividend be made, it be large enough to cover the entire amount of what may be fairly considered and adjudged as our 'surplus earnings' and conditioned on the agreement of the Rhode Island Hospital to accept this dividend in stock as in full satisfaction of all claims and demands under our charter or under an agreement with this Corporation dated September 4, 1874 and also that on receipt of stock from this dividend said agreement and all our obligations under it shall be fully canceled."

The amount decided on was one hundred shares of stock adjudged to be one-third of the surplus earnings. This was considered to be a "full and final extinguishment of all present, past or future claims and demands of the said Hospital upon this Company except as stockholders whether such claims and demands have arisen or may be thought to arise under the charter of this Company or under any part or existing contract or agreement between the said Hospital and this Company." In this way, thirteen years after the founding of the Trust Company, with the approval of both corporations, adjustment of the original agreement was made between the Rhode Island Hospital Trust Company and the Rhode Island Hospital.

The Hospital now became one of the large stockholders of the Trust Company and remains so to this day.

The corporation named for the Hospital and founded as a trust company retained its name which in the decades ahead was to become a household word in Rhode Island.

Other changes, due to resignations, deaths, and additions to the staff, were taking place in the Bank in the second decade. In 1881 Caleb Fiske Harris died. He had been a member of the Board of Directors for twelve years. Charles H. Sheldon, Jr., the Secretary, resigned the same year. He had held that position for ten years. The greatest change, however, was caused by a letter from the President, Mr. Binney, written in November of that year, in which he said that he would not be a candidate for office again.

Seekonk River, Washington Bridge — 1885, looking north from East Providence

Therefore, at the Annual Meeting in December, Alexander Farnum was elected President and Herbert J. Wells, Secretary. It was voted that "no Vice President be elected at this meeting."

Mr. Farnum was an author, a member of the General Assembly, a book collector, a bibliographer, and a popular lecturer. The *Providence Daily Journal* carried this notice in April, 1879: "Mr. Alexander Farnum will deliver a lecture on Roman art this evening at 7:45 o'clock in the room of the School of Design."

When Mr. Wells accepted the position of Secretary he left the Merchants National Bank where he had been employed for eleven years. He has often been quoted as saying later in life, "When I went to the Trust Company there were but ten employed by the Corporation including the President at one end and the janitor at the other."

A letter was sent to Mr. Binney expressing the regret of the Board of the Trust Company at his resignation: "the Directors . . . looking back upon what you have done and profoundly impressed with the great value of your service desire to place on record their high appreciation of the work you have performed and of the truly able and admirable manner in which you have discharged the responsible duties of President during all of your 14 years in office."

There were deaths in that period, too — William S. Slater, Alfred Anthony, head of the Board of Directors since its inception, Edward D. Pearce, and Amos Lockwood.

In January, 1883, Mr. Farnum became ill and requested a month's leave of absence. He was granted four months. Robert H. I. Goddard, the second generation of his family to serve on the Board of Directors, was elected President pro tempore by the Board to serve until June, 1883, when Mr. Farnum would return, and in that capacity, he wrote a note to the Secretary, Mr. Wells. A few instances of incivility on the part of Trust Company employees had been called to his attention. He mentioned these and then went on:

I wish to say most emphatically that in the future there must be no cause for unfavorable criticism in this respect. Let everyone understand that a knowledge of good manners is as important in a bank office as a knowledge of accounts; especially for those coming in contact with the public. Let it also be distinctly understood that a foolish question or remark from a customer will not be considered as an excuse for the slightest rudeness of manners. On the contrary, when a customer, or any person visiting the Banking Rooms, shows a lack of knowledge of business methods, a clerk is bound, all the more, to offer assistance or to impart information in a courteous and kindly spirit. We have an unusually large number of ladies among the patrons of this institution and it is . . . essential that the utmost consideration should be shown to them and that, if necessary, every possible aid should be extended to them, by the officers attending to their business wants. It is the little acts of kindness and courtesy which give to an institution of this kind character and popularity in the community. . . . I request you to inform all in the office of the contents of this letter and to be most vigilant in the future in detecting and instantly rebuking any instance of ungentlemanly or disobliging conduct. . . . In this connection I have a suggestion to make: If everyone is uniformly polite and courteous to his associates, he will be much more likely to preserve the same demeanor towards others doing business with the Company.

Banking, as one can see from this letter, has many facets.

In April, 1883, it was decided to discontinue the safe deposit business upon the expiration of the then existing contracts. Mr. Farnum returned in June but was absent again for a month in the summer, and at the Annual Meeting in December of that year the office of Vice President was again created. Mr. Wells was elected Vice President, as well as Secretary. An interesting postscript was added to the minutes of the same meeting: "November 18, 1883 at noon (being Sunday) a change of time was generally made throughout the country, being for this city that of the 75th Meridian west from Greenwich and occasioning a stoppage of clocks for about 15 minutes, the new time being that much slower." This was, of course, the establishment of Standard Time, or, as it was called in the beginning, Railroad Standard of Time.

The following spring, in May, 1884, there was a financial panic in New York, the most disastrous one since 1873, the year the Spragues failed in Rhode Island. The panic was the result of a shrinkage of values unheralded by the financiers. The New York banks fared badly; the repercussions were felt all over the country and were a source of anxiety to the officers of the Trust Company.

It was just at this time that the Bank suffered a stern blow in the death of its ailing President, Alexander Farnum. Following his illness of the year before he had returned to his duties. He presided at the April meeting of the Board but died before the May meeting. That the blow was not entirely unexpected can be seen from the minute adopted at the May meeting: "For the first time in the history of this institution the death of a chief executive officer must be recorded. On Sunday, the eleventh of May, Alexander Farnum, President of this Company, died at his home on Aborn Street. The members of this Board have for months watched with apprehension and sorrow the progress of the disease which has thus terminated in death; and they now desire to record their profound sense of loss and their sincere appreciation of the valuable, faithful and efficient services which Mr. Farnum rendered to this Company."

Mr. Farnum's death was a great shock to the entire personnel of the Bank, but the Board of Directors rallied, and Herbert J. Wells, Vice President and Secretary, was promoted to the office of President in June, 1884. Mr. Wells had been in the banking business since the age of eighteen, and his family had long been identified with banking in Rhode Island. His grandfather had been cashier of a bank in Kingston as early as 1818, and his father assumed the same position in a bank in Wakefield in 1835. Mr. Wells, as a matter of fact, was born in the building that housed the Wakefield bank. He was to hold the position of President of the Trust Company longer than anyone else before or since, and under his aegis the Bank was to grow and prosper far beyond the expectations of the original corporators. When he became Secretary in 1881 the resources of the Bank were reported as $7,721,132.29 by the State Auditor. When he resigned as President in 1919 the total assets, as found in the Bank Commissioner's statement that year, were $55,700,828.96. Late in life, Mr. Wells said that the responsibility of the presidency of Hospital Trust could not have been carried out with any success if not for the cooperation and wisdom of the Finance Committee (composed of Samuel M. Noyes, Amos C. Barstow, Royal C. Taft, and Robert H. I. Goddard when Mr. Wells first assumed the presidency). He talked about the officers: "To the ability of these men and their standing in the community is due in large measure the success of the Company today. Their efforts were supplemented by the ability of the membership of the general Board of Directors." He also revealed his management philosophy: "During the period of my whole connection with the Trust Company it has been the aim of the management to be of service to the community, to build safely for permanency rather than for present profit."

To serve with Mr. Wells, William H. Latham was elected to the office of Vice President (created by the Board's vote) and duties were assigned to him immediately. Under the direction of the President he was "to give special attention and supervision to the Bookkeeping Department, to the various trust accounts and to the care and management of the real estate and to the other property held in trust by the Company." This amount of special attention would be a crushing load for a Vice President in 1966, but it was not too much for him to cope with in that day when the position of fourth bookkeeper was still to be created and when the trust business was still not as important as the banking business. In 1877 a report of the Finance Committee which had examined the investments and securities held for the accounts of sundry estates listed fifty-five trust accounts. During the years that the Bank had its homes on South Main Street only 191 trusts were opened, or about eight a year. It was not until the early 1900's that the trust business would increase.

The close of the second decade of the Bank's existence coincided with

Herbert J. Wells
President 1884-1919

the deaths in June, 1886, of Mayor Doyle, of Providence, and of Bishop Hendricken. Mr. Doyle had been Mayor for eighteen years and was loved by the residents of the city, fifty thousand of whom went to view his body in City Hall. Bishop Hendricken was the first Bishop of the Providence Catholic Diocese and his body lay in state in the (then) new cathedral.

Rhode Island had grown during Thomas Doyle's mayoralty of the capital city of Providence. The industrial towns in the northern part of the state were becoming so populous that two of them, Pawtucket and Woonsocket, changed to the city form of government at this time. Providence, however, had been a city for almost half a century and in 1886 celebrated the two hundred

Early view Westminster Street, looking east from Empire

Mayor Doyle Monument, erected 1882

Railroad and the Cove about 1883

and fiftieth anniversary of the original settlement. The streets were gaily decorated, there was a balloon ascension, a trial of old hand fire engines, a parade of eighty-five hundred men in a military and civic procession, and the Honorable Thomas Durfee, Chief Justice of the Supreme Court of Rhode Island, delivered a speech. He concluded by saying, "We are on the threshold of a new half century ... Its 50 years ... advance invisibly through the mysterious region of the future, bringing with them the fortunes of the city ... She may not grow in the next half century so rapidly as in the last, but with her great natural advantages, her prestige of past success, her still unabated confidence, she has only to maintain her breed of noble men, her supply of intelligent, virtuous and enterprising citizens to make her continued progress assured."

These last words described not only Providence but the Rhode Island Hospital Trust Company as well. It was a summer of optimism inspired by the two hundred and fiftieth observance which caused the city and all the institutions in the city to review, to take stock, and to plan ahead.

37

CHAPTER THREE

Horse cars in Market Square 1892

1887-1896

By 1887 there was one other trust company in business in Providence and still another chartered but not yet organized. Competition was growing and would become keener still. In two years there would be four trust companies in the city and in a decade there would be six. One historian says that the "small banking capital of the trust companies, their liberal charter powers and the facilities which they could offer to depositors, drew to them a rapidly growing deposit account." Because of this and also because the President, Mr. Wells, had pointed out to the Board of Directors as early as 1884 that there was no stopping place between $500,000, the original authorized capitalization, and $1,000,000, a resolution was adopted by the Board in 1887 to investigate the possibility of increasing the capital stock "in view of anticipated competition in the business and the increasing demand for the stock of this Company." And so, in the spring of 1887 the capital stock of the Company was increased to $1,000,000, the limit authorized by the charter.

The following year a great step in the evolution of modern banking was made: a clearing house was established in Providence. A committee, of which Mr. Wells was a member, had worked hard to bring this about. Previous to this the inter-bank facilities consisted of a clearing system centered around the Merchants National Bank and the National Bank of North America, but in July, 1888, the clearing house was formed with thirty-four member banks. The Rhode Island Hospital Trust Company was number 33 of this group. The checks of the Company still bear the number 33 in the right-hand corner prefixed by a number 57, the number by which all Rhode Island banks are listed in the "Numerical List" of the American Bankers Association Blue Book. To any bank in the country "57-33" means the Rhode Island Hospital Trust Company. In addition to these two numbers there is also nowadays the number 115. The first 1 stands for the Federal Reserve District and the second 1 for the Reserve Bank serving the District; the 5 is used for sorting purposes, to facilitate the separating of items received for sorting by state. The check routing symbols plan was developed by the American Bankers Association and the Federal Reserve Banks to facilitate the sorting of checks to be collected through the Federal Reserve System. The first meeting of the Clearing House Association (now the Providence Clearing House Association) was held at Lyceum Hall, 62 Westminster Street, on February 2, 1888, at 11:00 A.M. and the articles of association were soon published. Article 2 stated that "The object of the Association shall be the effecting at one place the daily exchange between the several associated members and the payment of the balances resulting from the exchanges." In simpler language, a clearing house is the place where settlement is made of intra-bank debits and credits arising from checks, postal money orders, and bond coupons, a place where member banks meet and exchange checks. With the offsets of debits and credits they settle for large aggregate amounts of exchange by rather small balances. The hour set for making exchanges was 11:00 A.M. Initially they met at 27 Market Square, in rooms formerly occupied by the National Eagle Bank. In 1966 the Clearing House meets several times a day in the Phenix Bank Building on Exchange Street.

One of the original stockholders of the Trust Company and a member of the first Board of Directors died in the spring of 1889. Zechariah Chafee's death was mourned by men everywhere in the state, and one of the finest tributes paid his memory came from one of his legal advisors, Benjamin Thurston. "A personality," he said, "as unique as it was impressive has been taken from that elder group of men among us who represent the steady-going, methodical pace of the last generation. A character admirable for its masterly strength and yet lovable for its womanly gentleness, one in which there was well-blended the uncompromising force of intellect with the softening restraints of the heart."

As the century drew to a close many things associated with it were disappearing. The district of Narragansett was taken from South Kingstown and made into a town. A few years later Central Falls was separated from Lincoln and incorporated as a city. Providence, too, was undergoing a dramatic change. After years of discussion it was finally decided to fill in the cove, that body of water once covering almost all of downtown Providence. A beginning was made in 1889. There was great agitation for a new State House, a matter which had been discussed off and on ever since 1846 because the State House on North Main Street was inadequate.

In its way the Rhode Island Hospital Trust Company contributed to this changed physical look of the city. In the fall of 1889 one of the members of the Board of Directors, Royal C. Taft, reviewed the possibility of obtaining a new site for the office of the Company. The Finance Committee presented for consideration a proposition for the purchase of an estate on Westminster Street. A motion was then made and passed that the Finance Committee "be and hereby is authorized to purchase at a cost not exceeding $130,000 the estate known as the Sabin Estate, Westminster Street, this city." The stockholders at their Annual Meeting a few weeks later voted that the Board of Directors "be authorized in their discretion to construct on the location upon Westminster Street recently purchased of Charles Sabin a building for the use of this Company as a banking house and also for conducting a safety deposit business as

Cathedral of Sts. Peter and Paul, consecrated 1889

Colony House (presently district court), completed 1762

authorized in its charter." This facet of the banking business had been discontinued in 1883, but in April, 1891, the President suggested that the Board execute its discretion and take some action regarding it, and the Board voted to resume the safety deposit business as soon as possible after the completion of the new building.

By October, 1890, considerable progress had been made on the new building, and it was hoped that work would continue all winter with the building covered over. It took another year, however. It was not until November, 1891, that the Finance Committee was "authorized and directed to remove the offices and business of the Corporation from their present location to its new banking house designated as 15 Westminster Street, Providence, whenever the Building Committee shall give notice to said Finance Committee that the said banking house is completed and ready for occupation." A notice was then inserted in the newspapers: "The Rhode Island Hospital Trust Company will occupy its new banking house at 15 Westminster Street on and after Monday, November 30, 1891. E. S. Clark, Secretary."

On Tuesday, December 1, 1891, the Annual Meeting was held in the new banking house. The President reminded the Board that the first meeting of the corporation had been held on the same site (in the old Horse Guards' Armory), that William Binney was the one surviving original corporator, and that of the Directors elected at that organizational meeting in 1867 only two were present at the first meeting in the new banking house on Westminster Street: Amos C. Barstow and Christopher Lippitt. The President also reported that on June 1, 1874, the day the Trust Company moved from 37 South Main Street to 60 South Main Street, the capital stock was $500,000 and the total assets were $6,177,000. As of November 30, 1891, the day before the first meeting in the Westminster Street building, the capital stock was $1,000,000 and the total assets $10,619,000.

The newspapers gave the new building a great deal of space. They described it in detail: "A handsome yet unobtrusive exterior"; "Dignified architecture"; "Home of vast financial interests." "There is a dignity and an air of solidity about it," the *Providence Daily Journal* account read, "which well become the premises of a corporation which is enterprising and conservative." The stress was on quiet elegance and comfort. The façade was of pink granite with side and rear walls of brick and terra cotta tiling. The building was four stories high in front and three in the rear. The Westminster Street front was Romanesque, the entrance an arched double doorway with three polished granite columns on either side. Stairways from the vestibule descended to the

Safe Deposit Department and ascended to the main floor which was two stories high and had a mosaic floor. The vaults in the Safe Deposit Department were wired by the Rhode Island Electric Protective Company, the firm still handling this facet of the safeguarding of valuables for the Bank in 1966. The Rhode Island Safe Deposit Company had proposed to Hospital Trust to rent the Safe Deposit Department and manage it, but the Board of the Trust Company decided that "it was inexpedient to change ... plans respecting the Safe Deposit business," and in May a committee was appointed to supervise this department. A verbal contract (all that was needed in the simple days of the nineteenth century) was made with the Corliss Safe and Vault Door Company for a safe deposit vault, storage vault doors, and for a vault and safes required for the main floor.

In the first years there were no printed forms for use in the Safe Deposit Department. Orders for renewals of safe deposit boxes or for storing trunks, silver chests, or "grips" came to the Bank written on ruled paper, on printed letterheads, on post cards, and even on black-edged mourning paper. They were mostly handwritten, but after 1895 some typed orders began to appear. The letters were all folded lengthwise with the name of the customer and the date noted on the outside.

The section of downtown Providence where Hospital Trust was now located was to become the center of the banking interests of the city. References can be found to Westminster Street, east of Dorrance, as "Bank Street." The Rhode Island Hospital Trust Company was one of the most influential of the financial institutions to be established there.

Across the river from the Trust Company the Providence Cable Tramway line over College Hill to Red Bridge was opened in 1890, a great improvement over walking up this steep hill.

Progress was now being made on the State House, too. A few weeks after the new building of the Bank opened, the plans for the State House were placed on exhibition in Sayles Hall, at Brown University. Ground would not be broken until 1895, however, and the building would not be completed until 1901.

The year after the Bank moved to Westminster Street was a good year, and the annual business review in the *Providence Daily Journal* reported that a "gratifying improvement was made during the year of 1892. The greatest gain scored in the last six months. Cotton goods industry in splendid condition. Woolen mills active and show a decided gain. Foundry and iron work good. Much building in the suburbs. Retail trade excellent."

At the end of a year in the new building it was reported that there were 134 trust accounts representing property inventoried at almost $3,000,000. There is an interesting memorandum on the trust work issued that year. The President stated in it that he had watched the growth of that department hoping for an increase in business and a showing of larger profits. He wrote:

Ours is the oldest incorporated trust company in the state, yet possibly it is too early at this time to expect the full development of this part of our business. Up to this time,

Early view Westminster Street at Franklin

however, the revenue derived from this branch of our business is not commensurate with the expense and responsibility connected with its administration ... To give an idea of the management of these accounts it may be stated that a large proportion of the time of the Vice President and the entire time of one clerk is given to this department, as well as more or less of the time of the Secretary and the President. We are in almost daily communication with counsel as our action often involves the coming generation or the "remainder men." The question of taxation is a source of anxiety, the correspondence is considerable in volume and demands great exactness in making clear statements to the cestuis and even in the bookkeeping consultation with our attorney is frequently necessary to determine how to make proper entries.

That same year the total assets of the Bank were almost $14,000,000.

The feeling of prosperity was dissipated when a severe financial panic developed during the summer of 1893. There were two principal causes for this: one, the silver question, that is the free coinage of silver, and, two, the prospective changes in the tariff laws where some items would be placed on the free list. As a result many banks closed their doors, some temporarily, some permanently. The Trust Company took note of the panic and at the meeting of the Directors in August the President stated that due to the scarcity of currency it would probably be necessary to issue certified checks in large numbers to several customers for use in payrolls. He, therefore, asked for and received the authority to designate "one or more clerks temporarily to certify checks in view of a prospective demand for certification of a large number of small checks." At the next meeting a month later he reported that it had not been found necessary to sell any of the United States Bonds owned by the Company, and also that certified checks for use in payrolls had been used by only one of the Bank's customers. The monetary panic did not abate, and the President was authorized to notify the depositors in participation accounts that the usual dividend of 4 per cent would be payable in November, 1894, but that if low rates for the use of money continued "the Board may be compelled to reduce the rate of dividend on these accounts from and after that date." It was, and the dividend due and payable on and after May 10 was cut to 3.5 per cent. The participation deposits had increased greatly over the years, but the increase in the state tax and the difficulty in securing profitable investments pointed to the fact that a retardation of the growth of this part of the Bank's business should take place.

During the financial panic of that summer of 1893 there were large withdrawals from banks everywhere resulting in the suspension of several banks in the state. It was, therefore, suggested at the Annual Meeting of the Trust Company that the notice of withdrawal be reviewed because if there were a "sudden and increased demand on 'call' deposits it might prove embarrassing." Two means were suggested to combat this eventuality. The first that "the dividends on all accounts above a certain sum shall be one-half per cent less than those paid on smaller accounts," and the second that "the large depositors be required always to give a definite notice of considerable length before the withdrawal of their accounts." By adopting these suggestions it was hoped the number of "call" deposits would be reduced.

To assist in another way a contribution to the Republican National Committee of $2,000 was made in 1896. This contribution, according to the minutes of the Board of Directors, was "to aid in the defeat of the candidate of the party which in its platform has declared for the debasement of the currency, the overthrow of the Constitution and the letting loose upon society the most abhorrent forces of disorder and mob violence, thereby endangering the interests of this institution." These strong words referred, of course, to William Jennings Bryan who was the advocate of the unlimited coinage of silver. It was Bryan who, at the Democratic National Convention in Chicago in 1896, delivered the famous speech in support of the free coinage of silver: "You shall not press down upon the brow of labour this crown of thorns; you shall not crucify mankind upon a cross of gold." This speech brought him the Democratic nomination for the Presidency the following day.

The third decade in the Bank's history was coming to an end. The Trust Company now had a magnificent banking house. The decorating of the new building had finally been completed in the summer of 1894 and the Building Committee, appointed in 1890, had been discharged. Assets were at an all-time high — almost $16,000,000 — and yet in his Annual Report for 1896, Mr. Wells, the President, mentioned two events of national importance that had disturbed the business interests of the country. They were the Venezuelan proclamation and the Presidential campaign. The former item referred to President Cleveland's message to Congress in December, 1895. England and Venezuela had been arguing for a long time over the boundary line between British Guiana and Venezuela. Cleveland addressed Congress on the matter and said bluntly that he thought Great Britain's attitude was an attempt to control Venezuela. He suggested that a United States Commission study the matter and report on it. Great Britain finally accepted arbitration but for a while the situation was grave. The latter with its silver issue was also disturbing.

On a local level Providence in the early nineties was concerned with a new franchise tax. In 1891 the legislature had passed an act authorizing cities and towns in Rhode Island to grant exclusive franchises for the use of streets

"Old Mount Hope," favorite
of thousands of excursionists

Union Railroad (horse car) Depot — Market Square 1894

for the transmission of messages or power or the transportation of passengers, subject to an annual tax not exceeding 3 per cent of gross earnings. That year the city entered into a contract with the Providence Gas Company under the terms of an annual tax, and in 1892 the Narragansett Electric Lighting Company was granted an exclusive franchise for lighting the streets. The Providence Telephone Company also came under the tax that year.

In the Bank a historical oddity remains from this decade. It is a table called "Classification of Ladies Accounts Including Personal and Those Controlled by Ladies as Treasurer, Guardian or Administratrix." Today women are not only customers of the Bank, but they are active, articulate stockholders as well. In the 1800's, however, it was evidently a step forward to have them as customers.

Progress came in other ways, too, to the city and to the Trust Company. Electricity was being used more and more. Electric trolleys now replaced street railways, electric elevators were being installed in downtown buildings, and a system of electric signals was set up in the Bank to connect the various floors with the central police station.

In the 1890's, quite suddenly, the Bank doubled its trust business. Many of these accounts were charitable trusts, the handling of which laid the foundation for Hospital Trust's fine reputation in the management of charitable and institutional accounts. In 1896 the trust accounts represented property inventoried at about $6,000,000. In 1892 the comparative figure had been not quite $3,000,000. In those early days there was carried on the books "Trust #3," a trust for Providence Children's Friend Society provided for in the will of Charles Potter. This account is still open and active for the Children's Friend and Service. "Trust #4," established by Benjamin G. Pabodie for the Home for Aged Women, is still an open account. Also, at the end of its third decade the Rhode Island Hospital Trust Company had become agent for several organizations, among them the Providence Public Library, Brown University, the Shelter for Colored Children, and the Rhode Island Hospital. It had developed by then the facilities for handling a great diversity of business. The Safe Deposit Department had done well, too, earning its expenses during the first year of operation.

Growth showed everywhere — in the Bank, in the city of Providence, and in the country as a whole. The United States was becoming more active in the field of foreign relations and now took a long look at the revolt in Cuba against Spain. Since Jefferson's time it had been said over and over again that Cuba must not fall to any other nation if Spain relinquished it. During 1897 repressive measures were being carried out involving grave commercial injury to the United States and the situation became serious. Life and business were to be disrupted everywhere in the war that was to come, and the Rhode Island Hospital Trust Company, founded at the *end* of one war, now was for the first time to conduct its business *during* another war.

Cable cars at foot of College Hill about 1898

CHAPTER FOUR

State House — cornerstone laid 1896, delivered to state 1904

1897-1906

It was evident from all reports that war with Spain was inevitable. In February, 1898, the *Maine* was blown up and in April the President of the United States issued a proclamation calling for volunteers. Recruiting offices were opened in Providence, Newport, Pawtucket, Woonsocket, and Westerly. A second call for volunteers came on May 25 and the next day the First Rhode Island Regiment, United States Volunteer Infantry, left the state. During May and June many clerks in the Trust Company volunteered for military service and went to Camp Dyer at Quonset Point for training. At the June meeting of the Board of Directors of the Bank the President, Mr. Wells, stated that there "would doubtless be an increase of expenses the coming summer due to the employment of extra help during the absence of clerks in military service."

The General Assembly appropriated $150,000 to provide for military and naval expenses; Rhode Island filled her first quota of 720 men and also formed the Rhode Island Sanitary and Relief Association. And yet, with all the war excitement, business at home proceeded as usual. Hospital Trust secured the new State House loan, but in October, 1898, the Vice President of the Bank reported that the General Treasurer of Rhode Island, contrary to custom, "had deposited with another banking institution the proceeds of the $800,000 State House bonds recently purchased by this Company," it being stated by the General Treasurer that the rate of interest paid on said money is to be 3.3 per cent. This was a blow, but the rate of interest on call deposits that year at the Bank was 3 per cent and could not be raised, and an 1872 law, "Of the State Treasury and the Officers thereof," reads: "He shall deposit subject to his order, for the use of the State, all the funds of the State received by him in such safe and responsible banks either in Newport or Providence or in the Rhode Island Hospital Trust Company as will give the greatest rate of interest therefor." There was nothing the Trust Company could do about the situation, but some action was taken concerning another transaction earlier that year. The Bank had been assessed a tax on the premium of United States bonds and, as Administrator, brought suit to recover the tax. This was a test case and "judgement was rendered enabling this Company to recover from the city the full amount of tax paid under protest. This established the law that the premium of United States bonds cannot be taxed in this state." This law is still in force in 1966.

By this time the trust business had increased to the extent that additional meetings of the Finance Committee were necessary for the consideration of the accounts. In December, 1898, Mr. Wells addressed the Board of Directors:

You are aware, gentlemen, that the executive duties of the Board of Directors are performed by the Committee of Finance ... It is my pleasure to state that today the Honorable Royal C. Taft has completed 25 years of continuous membership on the Finance Committee. During that entire period our Company has had the benefit of his unfailing memory, his wide acquaintance with men and affairs, his ripe experience and his good judgment. On your behalf, gentlemen, I beg to extend to Governor Taft congratulations and thanks for the long and valuable services he has given to this Company. [He was to remain on the Board until his death in 1912.]

The next year Robert H. I. Goddard completed twenty-five years on the same committee and was praised for his "long, efficient and zealous service to the Rhode Island Hospital Trust Company." (There would still be a Goddard on the Board in the centennial year.) The Finance Committee was a hard working one for it was the standing Executive Committee of the Board of Directors provided for in the by-laws. It laid the foundation for and built up a trust company whose reputation is second to none. If, by its conservatism, it may have delayed the payment of large dividends, still the surplus it built up and the high quality of assets it developed contributed to the prosperity which the Bank now enjoys.

The year 1898 was the year Christopher Lippitt died. He was the last survivor of the original Board of Directors and had served for thirty-one years. Born on Lippitt Hill in Warwick, he became one of the foremost cotton manufacturers in Rhode Island and owned the Lippitt, Phenix, and other mills.

The closing year of the century waxed and waned. There was a notation in the minutes of the Annual Meeting in December: "The typewriter, various janitors and watchmen to be appointed as heretofore by the President." The use of the word "typewriter" to designate the man who operated the machine is interesting. It was only in 1878 that E. Remington & Sons, gunmakers, of New York, began to manufacture typewriters and in 1898 "typewriter" not only referred to the machine but also to the person who operated it.

52

At the turn of the century the factories in Providence and elsewhere in Rhode Island were humming. Throughout the state there were 255 establishments engaged in jewelry manufacturing and allied work. Of these, 97 per cent were located in Providence. There were factories where hair cloth, files, and wood screws were made. There were the great textile mills; within a thirty-mile radius of Providence was the largest textile center of the country. One historian expressed his feeling about Rhode Island this way: "The work of Gorham, Sharpe and the textile leaders Knight, Goddard and Lippitt is not finished. Wants beget wants; as American life advances more skill and organizing power will be furnished by the New England manufacturers. Is there not good reason to believe that Providence will continue to develop satisfactorily as a well-rounded industrial community?"

Providence did and as manufacturing increased in the northern part of the state the population did, too. Since business centered in the north, Providence soon grew to be five times as populous as any other city in the state. Therefore, in 1900 the May session of the General Assembly, which had always taken place in Newport, was abolished, and Newport was no longer considered a state capital. Up to this time Rhode Island had had two capitals, now Providence was the only one. All sessions of the General Assembly were to be held in Providence, and the first of these to be convened in the new State House met on the first day of the new century, January 1, 1901, at which time the state flag, adopted in 1897, was displayed.

In 1900 the Company took an option on some property, the Alexander and Daniel Griswold estate, which adjoined the Bank on the west and numbered 17-23 Westminster Street, running through to Exchange Place. The Board of Directors voted to avail themselves of the option and authorized the President to purchase the property. A rail fence was erected on the estate and at a special meeting in January, 1901, the Board took under consideration the improvement of the property.

In March a Building Committee was appointed to "proceed at once to the construction of a new building for the Company's use upon Westminster Street-end lot of the Griswold estate . . . and the remodelling of the present office building and a new safe deposit vault." The business of the Bank had more than doubled since it had been moved to Westminster Street and more room was needed. The contracts were signed by August, and the specifications required that the builder would arrange his work so that the officers need not be out of the building for more than sixty days. Work was begun in July, 1901, and during the construction, until the completion of the project in October,

54

1902, the Directors met in the Merchants National Bank. Another story was added to the banking house and a five-story addition was erected.

It must have been an upsetting time as proved by an appropriation of $5,500 at the beginning of 1903 "for distribution in gratuities among the officers (except the President), clerks and employees in recognition of the patience and loyalty shown by them in the trying circumstances attending the reconstruction and enlargement of the banking house." By the time the gratuities were

Old Slater Mill, first cotton spinning mill, now a museum, built in 1793

distributed the building was completed and occupied. Just about the time it was finished a banker from Kansas came to Providence on a visit. He was shown the three leading trust companies and was so unimpressed by their appearance that he patronizingly inquired about their capital and resources. The answer amazed him. He was astounded at the "humble and unpretentious type of banking house in Rhode Island." And yet the three banks he saw were the show places of the state.

The increase in space and facilities at the Trust Company brought an increase in business. By 1902 over 1,000 safe deposit boxes were rented and there were 175 trust accounts representing property inventoried at $9,969,385.67. Gross earnings for the Bank for the year 1902 were $953,789.77. This reflected the prosperity in the state.

With its new building the Rhode Island Hospital Trust Company fitted into the bustling life of the community. By March 28, 1903, the offices of the Company had been moved to the new structure, the actual cost of which was just over $281,000. The third, fourth, and fifth floors were rented, and the banking rooms were found to be comfortable and suitable for the expanding business. Trust accounts were up to 185, representing $10,000,000 worth of property, and the President's Annual Report for 1903 stated that "the volume and detail of our business constantly increases. A considerable portion of the time of the higher officials is necessarily taken up in conversations with important customers and as the business enlarges more and more time is thus consumed. In the near future some readjustment of the duties of the principal officers or possibly an addition to their number must be made, in order that they may give more important matters the deliberate survey and attention which they require and to which they are entitled." A trust officer had still not been appointed, but the time was fast approaching when an officer would be placed in charge of the Trust Department.

In the Annual Report for 1904, Mr. Wells spoke particularly about the trust business, about the diversity of accounts (guardianship, administration of estates, executorships under wills, etc.), and said that in addition the Bank was receiving from living individuals "an increasing number of what may be denominated as 'agencies' for the care of property for longer or shorter periods" and from charitable and philanthropic corporations "the care and investment of properties where treasurers of those institutions either preferred not to have the custody of the numerous securities or ... where they prefer that the Rhode Island Hospital Trust Company shall manage all of their financial business." He also stated that the Trust Department "absorbed much time and

Preston H. Gardner (1884-1947)
Elected Trust Officer, 1905; Vice President, 1912; Chairman of the Board, 1936.

anxiety on the part of the officials of the Company, that the risks were considerable and the benefits still comparatively small."

The first absorption of a bank by Hospital Trust occurred in 1904 when it acquired all the shares of the First National Bank. The business of the First National was brought to Hospital Trust and that bank closed, the first of many banking institutions to be absorbed by the Trust Company as part of its growth.

Much of the progressive development was due to the sagacity of Mr. Wells. By 1904 he had been President for twenty years. In June, the anniversary of his election to that office, he presented certain statistics showing the growth of the Company during those decades. Unfortunately, this report is no longer in existence, but the resources of the Bank that year of 1904 were reported at almost $25,000,000.

In 1905 Royal C. Taft resigned from the Committee of Finance and this was noted in the minutes.

Also, in 1905 the position of Trust Officer was finally created. Prior to 1905, William Latham and Samuel Dorrance, both Vice Presidents, had been in charge of trust accounts. Mr. Latham resigned in 1889; Mr. Dorrance retired in 1905, and his assistant, Preston H. Gardner, was elected Trust Officer and Assistant Secretary in charge of the Trust Department. He had come to the Bank in 1884 "for a few days, on trial." He was born in Swansea, Massachusetts, and had taught school for a short time before coming to the Trust Company. As Trust Officer he was given the care of the real estate and other property held in trust by the Company. One assistant from the Bookkeeping Department was assigned to him. From this date this department, which had grown slowly, began to flourish. There were, so to speak, years of laying the foundation for future trust work. By 1906 the number of accounts in this department had swelled to 275.

One of the most interesting accounts to come to the Bank during this decade was the Bradley Trust. George L. Bradley (and later his wife) left a will providing for the perpetual maintenance of a "charity" to be called the Emma Pendleton Bradley Home, named for their daughter. "Such purpose of ours," Mr. Bradley stated in his will, "arising from our special sympathy with those who suffer from disease because our child whose name said Home is to bear has been so afflicted through life. Out of this misfortune of our only child has grown the purpose and hope that from the affliction of this one life may come comfort and blessing to many suffering in like manner." The Home was to be established in the residence of the Bradleys, but upon their deaths the trustees decided the house was inadequate, and so it was sold to Providence College and property at the Veterans' Memorial Parkway and Pawtucket Avenue in East Providence, was purchased. The estate left to endow the Home was diverse. Mr. Bradley had owned, in partnership, a square mile of land in the Gogebic Range on the Michigan-Wisconsin border which was rich in deposits of iron ore and had leased it to a mining operator. For years warnings were issued that the ore

Emma Pendleton Bradley Home, East Providence

would run out, but it continued to yield revenue until 1965 for a total of almost seventy-five years. Mr. Bradley also had large interests in the Florida East Coast Canal and Transportation Company. This was a scheme to connect by canal various bodies of water near the East Coast and so make a continuous waterway from Jacksonville to Miami. The Trust Company as executor (with the approval of Mrs. Bradley while she was alive), because Mr. Bradley had expressed a desire in his will for the work to go on, completed the dredging. However, the canal was not profitable. It was finally sold to the United States government and is now maintained by the United States Army Engineers. All the land for right of way purchased by Mr. Bradley in connection with the canal was sold during the famous Florida land boom.

Mr. Bradley died in 1919, but the trustees of the estate had no authority to use capital of the endowment for the purpose of erecting a new building in East Providence. There was, therefore, a delay of several years until sufficient income had accumulated. Then, in 1929, a contract was signed and the building was completed in 1931. It is, as was the wish of the Bradleys, a memorial to their only child, Emma Pendleton Bradley. A psychiatric hospital for children, it was the first of its kind in the world. The Rhode Island Hospital Trust Company through its Trust Committee appoints the majority of the Board of the Bradley Home, and the estate is still administered by the Trust Company.

In 1906 the business of the American National Bank was transferred to Hospital Trust, the second bank to be absorbed by them. This same year the Bank took an option on the Vinton estate, from Westminster Street to Exchange Place, "in part to provide for the future growth of the Company and in part to aid in retaining the financial center in this locality." After the President, Mr. Wells, showed by comparative figures the growth of the Company's business since 1889, just before it moved to Westminster Street, it was voted to purchase the Vinton estate for $160,000.

Tremendous growth had taken place from 1897 to 1906, and yet, as always, the Bank officers were concerned with the community and the world. In April, 1906, the great earthquake in San Francisco occurred, and in May the expenditure of $1,000 for the sufferers from that catastrophe was voted, confirmed, and approved.

Progress had come in many forms in this decade as can be seen from the State Auditor's report of 1906. Twenty trust companies filed returns on June 30 of that year and the aggregate resources amounted to $128,942,363.14, over $13,000,000 more than the preceding year. The Trust Company's advertisements that year stated that capital was $1,000,000, surplus earnings $1,700,000.

Progress was also noted in the following sentence from the minutes of the meeting held on November 14, 1904: "Resolved that the general records shall be kept in a typewritten book."

A new century, new buildings, new methods signaled the dawn of new achievements.

"Old Turks Head" once known as "Whitman's Corner"

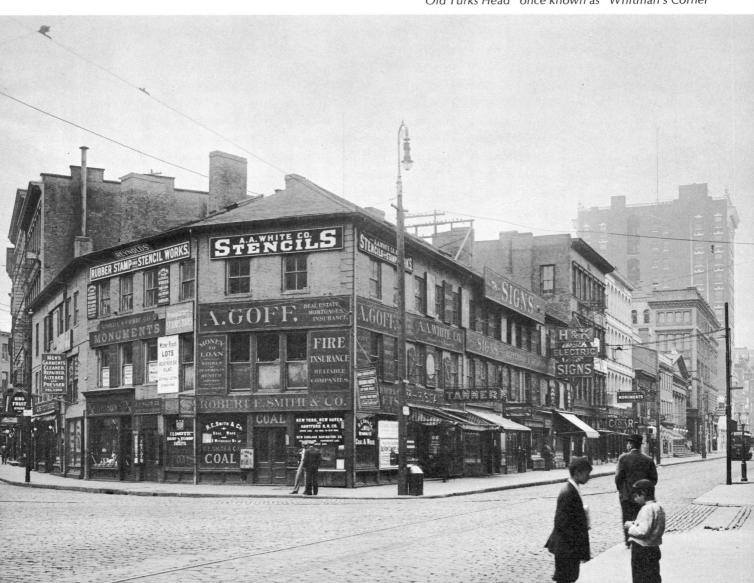

CHAPTER FIVE

Market Square, Turks Head building in background — 1913

1907-1916

On January 15, 1907, Herbert J. Wells, President of the Rhode Island Hospital Trust Company, called a meeting to consider the subject of the Vinton and Griswold estates, the newly acquired property of the Bank. There was a lengthy discussion about the increased banking facilities needed and then it was voted that "the President and two Directors be appointed a committee on plans to consider and report . . . upon the question whether it is desirable to improve by building or otherwise the Vinton estate, so called, either in whole or in part, including the Exchange Place property purchased from the Griswolds, with power to employ an architect or other assistance." This committee worked for almost six months and reported back in June with plans for a new building adjoining the banking house of Hospital Trust. Before any progress could be made, however, a serious problem arose in Providence and the nation: a financial panic.

Since the turn of the century the United States had been enlarging its economic functions. In 1903 the Department of Commerce and Labor had been created and its Secretary made a member of the President's Cabinet. This was necessary in view of the tendency in the United States at the beginning of the twentieth century to form huge combinations of capital and labor. Natural resources seemed to be passing into private possession and these resources were being exploited on the principle of "individualism by aggregations of capital which prevented effective competition by ordinary individuals." The panic of 1907 has been attributed by economists to the concentration of capital in a few hands. It started with the downfall of an attempted combination of a chain of banks, copper interests, and other enterprises by two operators on Wall Street and was followed by the collapse of the Knickerbocker Trust. In the fall of 1907 there was a sharp turn on the New York stock market which was actually a trap set for Charles W. Morse, a daring speculator, and his associates, including Marsden J. Perry, a Providence man, then First Vice President of the Union Trust Company.

On Thursday, October 24, 1907, there were wild rumors about Mr. Perry's whereabouts which alarmed Providence depositors, and they began a run on his bank. Mr. Wells invited certain gentlemen of Providence to attend a meeting in the Directors' Room of the Trust Company at 1:30 P.M. "to be one of a committee to take such action as is possible to restore confidence in the financial situation." The meeting was held with representatives of the Industrial Trust Company, the Union Trust Company, and the Rhode Island Hospital Trust Company all present. Bank examiners found the Union Trust solvent and to restore public confidence an examination of other banks was made. On October 25 the Union Trust did not open its doors and there were some drawings of savings from the other banks in Providence.

About ten banks and trust companies in Rhode Island were forced into liquidation in keeping with the national picture. By November 1 partial suspension was taking place all over the country and one source states: "Banking facilities were more completely interrupted than at any time since the Civil War." By December, at the Annual Meeting of Hospital Trust, a resolution was passed "that the thanks of the stockholders are hereby given to all the officers, clerks and employees of the Rhode Island Hospital Trust Company for their cheerful and faithful performance of the many additional and arduous duties incident to the failure of the Union Trust Company."

Eventually the Union Trust reopened and Mr. Wells distributed bonuses to Hospital Trust employees for their extra work during the disturbance. He addressed them in a body about their splendid cooperation, about the extra time and energy they had spent in order to keep up with the increase of business due to the emergency, and about their loyalty to Hospital Trust and to the President and his associates. He concluded by saying, "It was a long continuous strain upon the bodies and nerves of all of us; a long pull ... and I hope we may never have quite such a period of stress again."

Within a week or two the immediate panic was over in Providence, and the Bank began to work on the matter of an increase in the capital stock of the Company. It was decided to recommend such an increase to the stockholders at the Annual Meeting in December. If approved, application was to be made to the Rhode Island General Assembly for authority to increase the capital stock to an amount not exceeding $5,000,000. One other thing was accomplished in 1907. Section 10 of the charter of the Trust Company provided for the payment of certain profits of the Company to the Rhode Island Hospital. A final settlement had been made with the Hospital in 1880 but that section of the charter had not been repealed. Mr. Wells requested the General Assembly to repeal Section 10 of the Original Act of Incorporation of the Company as passed at its May session in 1867 (forty years before). The Hospital was asked to join in the request.

On the lighter side, in July, 1907, Providence held Old Home Week, a festival created to point out the attractions of Rhode Island and to lure former residents back to the state. To this the Bank contributed $1,000.

A new state banking law was passed in 1908. It provided regulations for the incorporation of banks, trust companies, and savings banks; prohibited unauthorized banking; established the office of Bank Commissioner; described the general powers of banks, savings banks, and trust companies; provided for returns and reserves. This made it necessary to revise the by-laws of the Trust Company. A committee was appointed to review the by-laws and in March, 1909, new by-laws were approved, confirmed, and adopted. Among other

One of many floats that were prepared for the Providence Old Home Week parade in July 1907.

things they provided for an increase in the number of Directors constituting the Committee of Finance from four and the President of the Bank, to not less than five or more than seven and the President; also, the Committee on Trusts was to be composed of the President and two members of the Finance Committee. (The first Trust Committee would not be appointed until 1910.) It was now also necessary to make an additional deposit with the General Treasurer of the state because in May, 1909, the capital stock was increased from $1,000,000 to $2,000,000.

That spring of 1909 William Binney, the first President of the Bank, died. A minute was offered:

To William Binney was confided the delicate task of organizing the Rhode Island Hospital Trust Company and of framing its early policies and to the successful realization and amplification of those policies is due its present commanding position. He suggested the word "participation," the value of which title has been demonstrated from the fact that it has been used by all other trust companies doing this class of business in this state. His study of other companies led him to embody in this Company the unusual powers of a bank, a savings institution and an incorporated trustee, a three-fold arrangement unusual if not unique for a financial institution in this country.

A portrait of Mr. Binney was given to the Bank by his widow and was hung on the wall of the Directors' Room. His death added a period to the first chapter of the Bank's history, a chapter which had really closed at the time of his resignation.

The next chapter was now more than half over with the celebration in 1909 of Mr. Wells's quarter century of service as the President of Hospital Trust. He was given a gold repeater watch and chain by the Board, which his grandson, Herbert C. Wells, Jr., Vice President in the Trust Department in 1966, still has in his possession. During Mr. Wells's presidency the Safe Deposit Department had shown continual growth and the trust business had become so important that in 1905 a separate department was formed and placed under the direction of an officer assisted by several clerks. The amount of commissions charged upon the income of the various trust accounts had increased from $13,200 in 1901 to $51,000 in 1909. Assets of the Bank increased during Mr. Wells's presidency from $8,500,000 to $41,000,000 and the number of employees from about ten to over eighty. A new building was erected in 1891 and enlarged in 1902.

In spite of the substantial growth of the Bank it was, by comparison with today's operations, still uncomplicated. The various "machines" in use included nine adding machines, eight typewriters, three canceling machines, two automatic cashiers, and two Protectographs. Electric fans and pencil sharpeners also came under the heading of machines. Data processing centers were still in the same category as trips to the moon. In the weekly reports from the Trust, Discount, Deposits, Loan, Real Estate, and other departments there were interspersed through the figures and percentages homely bits of news such as: "_____ is naturally left-handed but is counting bills right-handed with good results" or "there wasn't one of the examiners who could prove the foreign money; we were obliged to help them considerably."

There was a rash of counterfeit bills that year of 1909, and the Bank was forced to call in a Mr. Ahearn, of the United States Secret Service in Boston. The weekly report after Mr. Ahearn's visit stated, "Somebody is evidently passing these . . . on the street-cars."

The Bank family was small enough so that items like these were of interest, but it was large enough in point of work-load and number of customers so that the first telephone operator had to be hired in 1911.

Provisions had to be made in another way for the continued increase in business. The banking law of the state of Rhode Island limited the amount of deposits which could be held by any trust company to ten times the combined amount of its surplus and capital stock paid in. By the end of 1910 the deposits of the Company were approaching the limit prescribed by law. And so at the Annual Meeting in December the stockholders resolved that it was advisable to increase the capital stock from $2,000,000 to $2,500,000.

The year the capital stock was increased the Company was qualified to receive Post Office Savings Bank Deposits.

The increased trust business brought with it the care of real estate all over Rhode Island. The amount of commissions derived from the income of the various trust accounts was $76,200 in 1911; it had increased almost six times over that of the first year of business. The report on the Trust Department that year states: "At least once in the history of this Company a testator has died and we have settled his estate and paid out the trust to his beneficiaries. The beneficiary of the first estate thereafter has died and we have been called upon to administer the same property again." The value of good will of the Company was indicated by the increase in business and by the creation of trusts by those who formerly were beneficiaries under other trusts.

The city's activities expanded, too. Traffic conditions, for instance, in downtown Providence were so bad in 1911 that a transportation expert was hired. His recommendations included among other things the Exchange Place loops and turnouts for trolleys. A report of the day states:

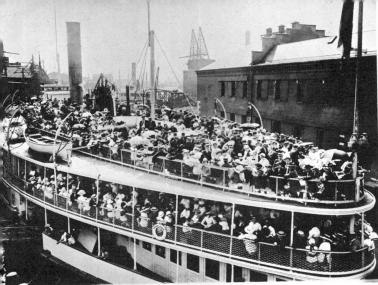

Excursionists ready for "a day on the bay"

Westminster Street at Union, about 1914

There is enough money in the Providence banks to rebuild the city in a much more costly manner if it were swept off the earth by a conflagration tomorrow. In a short time, however, there may be enough to build several such cities for the deposits are increasing in much greater ratio than the realty valuation. The national and state banks and trust companies for example more than trebled their deposits in the 10 years ending 1908 . . . The city is located in the most prosperous district in the United States and it has been estimated that one-twentieth of all the wealth in the country is within 50 miles of Providence.

In 1912 Royal C. Taft died. He had been a Director of the Bank and a member of the Committee of Finance for nearly forty years and from 1888 to 1889 he had served as Governor of Rhode Island. Many eulogies were delivered after his death and the spread on the minutes read in part: "He was called genial companion and friend, wise counsellor, foremost banker, distinguished citizen. He served faithfully his day and generation."

It was in the early years of this century that the National Citizens League of New England was formed for the promotion of a sound banking system, and it worked for the establishment of the Federal Reserve Act. Senator Nelson W. Aldrich, of Rhode Island, was the chief proponent for national monetary and banking reform. "The Aldrich Plan" was published in 1911 and three years later its principal provisions were used as the basis for the Federal Reserve System which was established to strengthen the United States banking system. Senator Aldrich was a Director of the Rhode Island

Hospital Trust Company from 1898 to his death in 1915. He served as a United States Senator from Rhode Island from 1881 to 1911 and as Chairman of the National Monetary Commission of 1908. He had a "powerful influence over tariff and currency legislation . . . He framed in large measure the Aldrich-Vreeland Act, which proved to be of inestimable value to the country. . . . These important contributions to the currency and banking laws of the country entitle him to rank as the great authority of his day upon the subject of finance." In 1915, the year he died, the Bank purchased the Washington Row property, planning to enlarge its headquarters.

This piece of land on the riverside had an interesting history. The Washington Row property plus twelve lots west of it to Exchange Street were once called the thirteen water lots, as well they might be. They were bounded by water on two sides: north by the Great Salt Cove and east by the Providence River. Prior to 1746 this land was Common Land in the town of Providence and in that year some of the men who owned the lots had wharves at the rear of their land, on the Great Salt Cove, and stores and houses on the south side fronting on the "Highway Going West From Great Bridge"— now Westminster Street. The Providence Washington Insurance Company had acquired lot number 13, right on the river, and when they erected the building known as the Washington Buildings, the name of the street in front of their door was changed from Westminster Row to Washington Row. By 1830 some of the cove had been filled in on the north, too, so that soon water lots would be an inappropriate name for this land which was really the northeast end of Weybosset Hill. The Washington Buildings, so imposing that visitors to Providence thought they must be viewing the State House or City Hall, was so named from the fact that it was the home of the Providence Washington Insurance Company, a new building erected in the 1840's (completed in 1846) around some of the previous buildings put up by this same company — therefore, Washington Buildings. Many of the old businesses of Providence were located at one time or another in this building.

The Committee on Increased Banking Facilities of the Rhode Island Hospital Trust Company was also authorized to acquire by lease or purchase the Lewis estate on Exchange Place, north of the Trust Company. It was leased in January, 1916, for a period of ninety-nine years. This committee saw the need of planning ahead for the next twenty-five years. They suggested a larger lobby and placement of the officers as near the entrance as possible, accessible to the public. They also suggested that the officers have rooms for consultation. They recommended that the Trust Officer and his assistant should be on the first floor and that the new building should be an office building, not merely a home for the Trust Company.

While the planning of the new building was going on and the purchase and leasing of property was taking place for the improvement of the physical plant, plans were being made which would result in great advantages to the personnel of the Bank, to the Bank, itself, and to the community. A pension system was adopted in 1914 "for the benefit of the clerks and employees and all or such of the officers of this Company as they deem proper." At the same meeting Mr. Wells, the President, read a paper on the occasion of the thirtieth

Brown University, founded 1764 — University Hall in background

anniversary of his election to that position. Many of the men he had worked closely with were dead: Robert Ives Gammell, Royal C. Taft, and Nelson W. Aldrich among them. Mr. Wells's work went on, however, careful and farseeing. At this Annual Meeting in December, 1914, Thomas H. West, Jr., of the St. Louis Union Trust Company, was elected Vice President.

The year 1914 was one of uncertainty because of the war raging in Europe and the low rates of interest. The war slowed down the political campaigns that year. In Providence the celebration of Brown University's one hundred and fiftieth anniversary was in the news. And one solution to the city's traffic problem was evolved with the completion of the East Side tunnel.

The next year employment was high since Europe was now looking to the United States for food, clothing, and munitions. The debt-ridden Providence trolley system (the Rhode Island Company) was reorganized during the period from 1915 to 1916 by Theodore Francis Green, one of five trustees running it for the New York, New Haven and Hartford Railroad. Spanish influenza raged in Providence and gatherings were banned for a time. Some of the employees of the Bank were going off to war, some were being trained at Plattsburg, some at Fort Greble. To replace the men going into service many more women were being hired. In 1916 Ann E. Fryer came to the Bank, one of the first women in the Bank's history to reach a position of high responsibility. She worked first as a secretary; then she had charge of the stenographic work in the Trust Department; then she went to the Personnel Department. She was never made an officer for in those days women were not elected officers of the Company, but in the opinion of those who remember her and her work, she made it possible for women to become officers now. She retired in 1942 and in a farewell article in the Bank's magazine, *Around the Clock*, the writer says, "the imprint of her character and her spirit and of all that she has done through the years for her girls will never leave those of us who have come under her guidance and who admire her deeply."

Another important event occurred in 1916. In February, five well-known local men asked the Trust Company to consider the formation of a community trust for charitable purposes. This type of trust had first been established in Cleveland, Ohio, in 1914. The Board of Directors agreed that it would be of great benefit to the community "by providing a permanent fund for assisting and promoting worthy charities and by securing, so far as human foresight is able, the preservation and proper application of the property given." "Therefore resolved," the minutes read, "that this Company will accept such a trust as this day presented under the name of the 'Rhode Island Foundation.' "

71

The basic idea of the community trust was not new. In 1814 Obadiah Brown, one of the leading merchants of Providence and the owner of a spermaceti works, had written a clause into his will setting aside a liberal sum for "such benevolent purposes as should be determined upon by certain trustees."

By the provisions of the Rhode Island Foundation the benefactions of the foundation are limited to Rhode Island, but "within the limits it possesses a wide latitude for helpful activities. It may assist permanent enterprises of a charitable or humanitarian nature, it may supply an emergency fund in time of sudden disaster ... it may establish means for the training of mind and hand and 'for the uplifting of heart and spirit.' " The Rhode Island Foundation "in purpose, in operation and in management is in every sense of the word a community enterprise, the provisions for whose maintenance and conduct are broad as well as secure."

Meanwhile a Building Committee had been appointed to have complete charge of the erection of the new building. The site for this building was considered by the Henry W. Cooke Company, real estate agents, "as good as any in the city" for a new building "for first class offices." This firm reported that there was "increasing inquiry for more office space in Providence." The Building Committee, therefore, proposed an eleven-story building. In November, 1916, the committee was authorized to proceed with the erection of this building based upon the U-plan.

The question of increased banking facilities was now answered with the purchase and leasing of property, the appointment of the Building Committee, and the approval of plans. A half century after its founding the Rhode Island Hospital Trust Company was erecting a handsome, tall building, but there was more than the physical plant to show for five decades of business. Perhaps the results of fifty years of assiduous work can best be illustrated by a letter received in 1911 by the President of the Trust Company. It was from one of New York's strongest banks and read: "I find on my desk this morning a copy of your statement as of October 31 which I have examined with very much interest. I desire to congratulate you upon the strength of your showing and the magnificent institution of which you are the head. The name of your Company is a synonym of strength and the very highest type of business methods."

Fifty years of steady progress had now been made and all the benefits of hard work — tangible as well as intangible — had come to the Rhode Island Hospital Trust Company. It had hewed to the line laid down by William Binney; it had borne out the prophecy made in one of its first advertisements in 1868: "So long as the direction shall remain in the hands of men of the character of those who now compose it," this advertisement read, "this Company will meet and satisfy a want which has never before in our community been met — safety and economy; ensuring these to people of small means in the management of their property, it will be a 'boon to the masses.' "

East Side Tunnel under construction — 1914

CHAPTER SIX

Lower College Hill — Bank in background — 1919

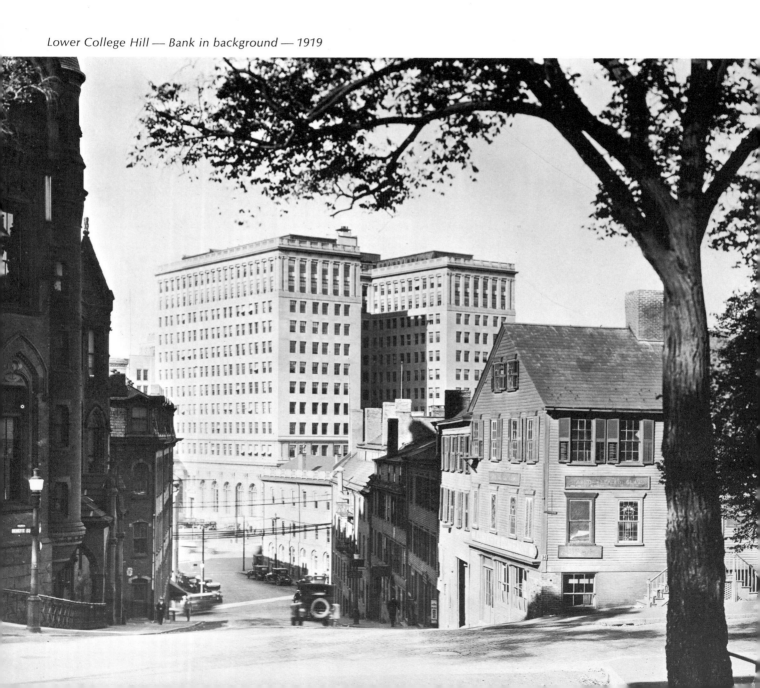

1917-1926

The first quarter of the year 1917 was crowded with world-shaking events. Every day the newspapers carried fearful headlines about the war in Europe: "Germany Declares a Ruthless Submarine War"; "Washington Staggered at Grave Issue Precipitated by Ultimatum"; "Relations with Germany Severed"; "U-boat Sinks American Steamer."

In Rhode Island the war touched everything and everyone. Brown University was raising funds for the American Ambulance Field Service; the Rhode Island National Guard was on duty at the Tin Bridge in Pawtucket, at the New Haven Railroad Tunnel, and at the drawbridge over the Seekonk River. Food prices were up, and since the bay was frozen from shore to shore, neither food supplies nor coal were being brought in by ship. When one of the Fabre Line boats did arrive in port, she displayed guns on her deck. At Washington and Aborn Streets a station was set up for recruiting National Guard members. People were asked to use less sugar, and in the spring to raise vegetables to help combat high food costs.

In spite of all the alarms — U-boats off the coast, enemy airmen overhead, spies — life went on. Providence College was granted a charter. A survey was made to improve trolley service at rush times when 124 cars an hour made the run on Westminster Street between Dorrance Street and Market Square. Daylight-saving time was urged for Providence, and on January 21, 1917, the *Providence Daily Journal* reported: "Washington Row, for many years the center of the city's commercial district, gives way before the march of progress. On its site will be reared the new home of the Rhode Island Hospital Trust Company." Most of Washington Row was empty by the time the Bank acquired and razed it. It was planned to continue the banking business as usual at 15 Westminster Street, which was south of the Washington Row property. When the first section of the new building would be completed, the Trust

75

Company would occupy it. Then the 15 Westminster Street building would be wrecked and the second section erected. The contractors and builders were to run into many difficulties because of the war, transportation problems, and labor conditions. A forty-foot annex to the west was planned for some future date, and the Safe Deposit Department was to have forty-five coupon rooms with a capacity of ten thousand boxes. The doors to the vault for this department, including frames, weighed nearly fifty tons each and arrived in April drawn by a team of eight horses. The earth excavated at the site was put in horse-drawn carts, although pictures taken at the time showed dump trucks, too. It was that era when horses and automobiles shared the streets.

Construction had barely begun when, on April 2, 1917, President Wilson asked the Congress to declare a state of war existing between the United States and Germany. As a direct result of this, at the meeting of the Board of Directors of the Trust Company that month, it was "voted, that any employee of this Company enlisting in the United States Army, Navy or National Guard, when called into service, be paid the difference between his present salary and his compensation from the Government and that his position with this Company be kept open until the next annual election . . . [and] that it be the policy of this Company to continue this action during the War."

At this same meeting it was decided to request the Secretary of the Treasury of the United States to designate the Rhode Island Hospital Trust Company a Government Depository, since on behalf of itself and its customers the Company "is making subscriptions to the United States Liberty Loan . . . and desires to receive deposits from the Government on account of said loan."

The war made it necessary for the Board of Directors of the Trust Company to discuss the matter of joining the Federal Reserve System. The President of the United States had urged the formation of the Federal Reserve System for all state banks and trust companies in order to consolidate the banking resources of the country during the world crisis. Senator Nelson W. Aldrich, of Rhode Island, who was a member of the Bank's Board of Directors for almost twenty years, had proposed in 1911 certain changes in the banking laws of the United States with a view to the creation of central reserves, a system adopted afterwards in the Federal Reserve Bank.

The functions of the Federal Reserve System for the first two years of its life were concerned largely with modifying banking practices in the United States and with organizing its own units. After war was declared, many companies filed applications to become members. Part of the wish to join was actuated by patriotism — to strengthen the government's accounts — and by the fact that the severe financial strain of the war would be most easily met by those banks which had joined, because the Federal Reserve provided "for a flexible currency system." Hospital Trust now decided to make application to join. The President, Mr. Wells, reported at the Annual Meeting that the "Company may enter the Federal Reserve System."

At the same meeting he noted that 1917 was the fiftieth anniversary of the founding of the Trust Company. "At the conclusion of the present calendar year," he said, "this Company completed a half century of business. The year has been a most eventful one. The entrance of our country into war has changed the current of many enterprises ... All of these matters have greatly confused and discouraged the financial affairs of the country." He mentioned the two Liberty Loan drives, the fact that men were assembling in the Army and Navy all over the country, that thirteen clerks had left the Bank and that women had been hired to replace them, and that $8,000,000 of subscriptions to the first

New building under construction during Liberty Loan drive

Arrival of new vault door

State Liberty Loan, or 39 per cent of the Providence total, went through the Bank's office. He reported that progress was being made on the new building, that concrete had been poured beginning in May and that it was hoped that they would occupy the first section in 1918. Total assets of the Bank at the end of 1917 were $61,940,359. The capital stock was increased that year to $3,000,000.

In 1918 the tempo of the war and precautionary measures increased. At the beginning of the year Providence residents were asked to share their coal with people who had none. Schools were closed because of the scarcity of this fuel. Guards were placed over all government property in Providence and Newport, and waterfront zones were set up from which aliens were barred.

By January, 1918, the Trust Company had qualified as an Agent of the Second Class for the sale of War Savings Certificates and Stamps. Other war business was conducted at the January meeting of the Board of Directors when the following resolution was passed:

Resolved, that all payments to men who have heretofore enlisted, been drafted or who shall hereafter enter the service, cease on and after each man has been in the pay of the Government for one year, it being understood that drafted men are to receive compensation on the same terms and under the same conditions as applied to enlisted men. Also that after the expiration of said one year, authority is hereby given to the President and Vice President to deal with individual cases in their discretion, making such payments as in their judgment each case may require to relieve his own or his family needs; also Be It Further Resolved that those who have entered the service be given first consideration for positions with this Company when returning from service either before or after the expiration of the war.

In March the application for membership in the Federal Reserve System was approved. Due to the facilities which the Federal Reserve supplied through Hospital Trust and its other member banks, Rhode Island industries rapidly adapted to the requirements of the war and to the floating of the immense government war loans.

Again, at the monthly meetings of the Board of Directors during the summer much of the business had to do with the war. Resolutions had been adopted in the fall of 1917, as mentioned above, to qualify the Company as a Government Depository. Mr. Wells reported at the meeting in August that the Company had been acting as Depository under the provisions of the Trading-with-the-Enemy Act but that since that appointment the powers of Depositories had been considerably increased and that a new designation had been sent for the Bank's acceptance. It was, therefore, "resolved that this institution accept the designation of Depository for the Alien Property Custodian dated the 30th day of July, 1918, subject to all the conditions and limitations therein contained."

One of the conditions was the posting of a bond "in favor of the Alien Property Custodian" and one of the Bank's functions under the new designation was to care for property belonging to aliens which had been claimed by the government. In the Trust Department, for instance, there were one or two agency accounts that belonged to aliens. The Trust Department, under the appointment of Depository, reported to the government on that property instead of to the alien-owner.

When the new draft law went into effect, later in the summer, the vote to pay those who enlisted in the Army or Navy was rescinded. The President stated that because of the draft "it seemed desirable to rescind votes heretofore passed relative to compensation to men in the service of the United States." The motion was made and passed "that the votes of April 10, 1917, January 8, 1918, and March 12, 1918, relating to the compensation to men in the service of the United States be and hereby are rescinded as to any employee who may hereafter enter the service."

Other business that summer included the election of members of the committee of the Rhode Island Foundation "to direct the application of the net income thereof" and decisions concerning the new Trust Company building. Some of these were "that rents for rooms on the second floor be not less than $2.00 per square foot, that no soda or sandwiches be sold in the stalls in the lobby, that for the present no rooms be rented either to dentists or doctors, that a barber shop located somewhere in the building is desirable." It was decided to add a "second position" to the telephone switchboard and to put one flagpole over the Washington Row entrance, the flagpole to be taken from the building then at 15 Westminster Street. The trolley wires were to be attached to the building rather than to poles which would have to be placed along the sidewalk. At the October meeting the President reported that "the successful removal of the contents of the old safe deposit vault into the new vault was accomplished on Saturday and Sunday, October 5 and 6, finishing Sunday about 9:30 P.M." The vault was open for business at 9:00 A.M., Monday, October 7, 1918. Section A (the northern half) of the new building was so near completion that fall that it was decided to hold the Annual Meeting there in December.

Before the time for that meeting, however, the Armistice was signed. On November 7 Providence went wild over a false report of the German surrender and on November 11 the state was in an uproar when official word arrived. The Governor issued a proclamation making the cessation of business legal and there was a Bank Holiday. The *Wall Street Journal* on November 13 stated: "The most stupendous, the most costly, the most destructive of all wars, involving a multitude of questions that are vital to civilization, has been brought to a close ... Advocates of a doctrine that might is right are now convinced of their error ... An overruling Providence has controlled the doctrine of men and nations and has provided for the betterment of the human race.''

As had been planned, the Annual Meeting on December 3, 1918, was held in the new building, although the Trust Company would not move in until January, 1919. The meeting took the form of a dedication and was a gala affair. W. H. P. Faunce, President of Brown University, delivered the dedicatory

Students entering Harkins Hall, Providence College, Chartered 1917

address. There was an inspection of the building from the roof to the vaults by stockholders and guests. President Faunce said in part:

Every building is a confession of faith, is a creed made visible. What we in our hearts believe gets itself uttered in the structures we erect ... What then does it say to the passerby? It says clearly and unmistakably that the greatest asset in modern business is character. ... This institution has had three homes before this one, all of them substantial structures. It has employed all known devices to protect its funds, but the confidence of a community has depended, not on strong boxes and brick vaults, not on timelocks and bars of steel, but on the men behind all possible equipment ... This building is not merely a place for the deposit of securities. It is a home under whose ample roof the savings of the poor, the bequests of parents to their children, the funds of corporations and educational and religious societies may be cared for by men who want to be something more than successful, who want to be serviceable to their generation. Such men have gathered in your Directors' Room for more than half a century. Such men will not fail in the centuries that are to come.

This dedicatory meeting was followed on January 17, 1919, by a supper for Directors, officers, and employees in the lobby of the new building. Again, many speeches were made and one in particular by the Reverend Arthur H. Bradford took the form of a "Creed for the Good Citizen of Providence." This began: "I believe that the place in which I live, while I live in it, should be regarded by me as the greatest place in the world, and as it gives me the best it has, it deserves to receive from me the best that I can give it."

A description of the main banking room was provided in the first issue of the *Netopian,* a monthly magazine of the Bank that would begin publication in April, 1920:

As a fitting home for the institution which more than half a century ago brought to Rhode Island what was then a more inclusive form of bank, we have a natural satisfaction in the building's dignity and beauty ... About 5,000 square feet in the center is devoted to public use. Customers' desks extend north and south from the information desk and are conveniently located. Easily accessible for all who have business with them are the officers and heads of departments. In this arrangement the Company's ideal of friendly business is well served. The beauties of the room are such as harmonize with its purposes. A quadrangle is outlined by 24 pillars that rise to a height of 34 feet supporting the entablatures from which the barrel-vault roof springs ... The room is admirably lighted by the large skylight and by windows that extend nearly the full height of the walls ... The design and decorations reflect the spirit of Italian renaissance ... The effect of the room as a whole is a rare combination of neutral richness and cordial warmth ... The building itself has a length of 189 feet on Washington Row and is 128 feet in depth. Its 11 stories carry it to a height of 174 feet. In general, its architecture has been pronounced a particularly fine example of the "American business type."

In May, just as the Bank settled into its new building, Mr. Wells, the

President, offered his resignation and asked for a leave of absence until it would become effective. He had guided the Trust Company through its years of growth on Westminster Street, through the war, and the construction of its new home. He had built, according to his successor, Thomas H. West, Jr., "an institution that is a credit to his city and state." Mr. Wells had served the Bank for thirty-eight years, thirty-five of them as President. His resignation was accepted on June 10, 1919, on the thirty-fifth anniversary of the day he became President. The corporation did not want to lose the benefit of his experience so it was recommended that the position of Chairman of the Board be created and that Mr. Wells be elected to that position. He was, therefore, elected Chairman of the Board of Directors and Mr. West was elected President in October.

Mr. West's father had been president of a bank in St. Louis. After graduating from Yale University, the younger Mr. West returned to St. Louis and founded with an associate the Broadway Savings Trust Company there. He later became Secretary of the St. Louis Union Trust Company, the largest in that city. He was a member of a Yale alumni committee established to secure funds for the building of the Yale Bowl. At the Annual Meeting in December, 1914, he was elected Vice President of the Trust Company. He headed all five of the state's Liberty Loan Campaigns, every one of which went "over the top."

One of Mr. West's first messages to the Board of Directors was that the Bank must departmentalize. The Trust Company was no longer the simple organization that had come into being in 1867. It had a Trust Department, a Commercial Banking Department, a Safe Deposit Department, and a Savings Department which was run as part of the Commercial Department. The nuclei of many new departments were there and with the tremendous growth of the Bank it was now necessary to formalize departments that in most cases were already working, but without titles.

In accord with Mr. West's suggestion several new departments were born. By 1922 there were a Mortgage and Real Estate Department, an Investment and Statistical Department, a Foreign Department, and an Agricultural Department. The Agricultural Department was established with the hope that it could help to make farming profitable in Rhode Island by cooperating with the farmer "on a basis similar to that afforded the manufacturer or merchant or any other business man," by offering a banking service embracing credit and information. It is interesting to note that Ernest K. Thomas, manager of this department, would resign in 1929 to become the Superintendent of Parks in Providence.

By 1923 there would be a Personnel Department and at that time the staff would number 238. Up to this time the Secretary of the Bank had done the

Thomas H. West, Jr.
President 1919-1936

interviewing and hiring; the Personnel Department would now take over that function.

About this time a Tax Division of the Trust Department was formed. Income tax service was to be given to persons who had trust accounts or were beneficiaries of trust accounts; it also handled federal, estate, and inheritance tax work on estates and trusts being administered by the Company; federal and state gift tax work; city and town taxes on real estate, and tangible and intangible property on estates and trusts. Within twenty-five years the Tax Division would report $50,000,000 worth of property to the city of Providence. (The assessment of December 31, 1965, which is the latest figure available at this writing, was for just over $108,000,000.) Income tax was then in its infancy for the foundation of a federal system of income tax was laid only in 1913 by the ratification of the Sixteenth Amendment.

When the *Netopian* appeared in April, 1920, it carried, in addition to the description of the banking rooms already quoted, a message from the President, Mr. West:

To the people of Rhode Island, the Rhode Island Hospital Trust Company takes pride in its new business home now fully occupied after many months of partial use. It has provided what it believes to be the most convenient and well-equipped trust company quarters to be found in New England, but our pride is not merely in the architectural qualities of building and banking rooms. It is because these give us a service plant that will multiply the Company's power to work with the community of which it has been so long a conspicuous part. A banking institution flourishes only in proportion to the service it renders. Our new home is not only testimony of the cooperation we have been able to give, it is evidence of still broader work toward which we look. With the experience of more than half a century on which to found new forms of utility, always adapting itself to the growing needs of the community, this Company welcomes the people of Rhode Island not only to its new building but to share in the use of its resources.

At this time the Building Committee in its final report listed the cost of the Head Office as $3,175,273.27. The report ended with a denial of the rumor that the Bank had built "at the most expensive time." The committee noted that it had been informed that month (November, 1920) that the structure would have cost $1,000,000 more if it had been erected in 1920 instead of in 1917. By the time this report was made, every office in the building was rented.

The Safe Deposit Department by the end of 1920 had 7,230 safes installed, of which 5,327 were in use. The Bookkeeping Department by that year required six automatic statement machines to compile the individual statements rendered to depositors. The Trust Department from 1905 to 1920 "had established a notable record in financial development, its business having doubled twice in that period; in some instances the same property coming to the Bank three times in different trusts, a tribute to the service performed and the business friendships this created." Frederic J. Hunt, who came to the Bank in 1916 and was in charge of the Trust Department for over a decade, has stated that the trust business was growing all over the country in the twenties and thirties due to the prosperity of the people and the sudden awareness on the public's part of the service available to them. Since the Rhode Island Hospital Trust Company was the oldest of the trust companies in New England, it naturally benefited from these conditions.

In 1920 for the first time the Bank did some business outside the walls of the banking house — providing a service that would be taken over in 1921 by a new Foreign Department, the first such department in any bank in the city. Providence was a terminal port for the Fabre Line and a point of entry for immigrants who were usually detained for an examination of their papers and for a literacy test after the boat docked. When they were ready to leave the pier, local agencies stepped in to assist them. The International Institute was represented, Red Cross conducted a canteen, and now, at the request of the Red Cross, the Rhode Island Hospital Trust Company sent a clerk to meet every ship for the purpose of exchanging money and rendering other financial aid. Unscrupulous money-changers had been taking advantage of the travelers' ignorance of American money. With the Trust Company on the spot, the newcomers received the same fair, courteous service that the regular customers of the Bank were used to. Sometimes the Trust Company's representative stayed on the pier until after midnight to discharge his duties and sometimes he met steamers on Sundays and holidays. This practice was to continue until 1930 when most passengers would be Americans and, in many cases, would disembark not in Providence, but in New York.

Not only had travel resumed between countries but international trade, too, was reviving. Because of this the International Acceptance Bank was formed in 1921. Its purpose was to encourage international business. The Rhode Island Hospital Trust Company was an original stockholder and was represented on the first Board of Directors by its President, Mr. West. Exports to foreign nations had to be paid for by imports from those nations. The International Acceptance Bank, therefore, was to consider the needs of the importer and exporter. It specialized in the granting of acceptance credits growing out of international trade and so rendered its stockholders a foreign service that could scarcely be expected of a bank engaged in other forms of banking. Clients of the Trust Company could obtain exact information concerning credit standing of prospective customers and general business and financial conditions in foreign countries. Documents involving shipping and payment received careful attention and detailed explanations of customs requirements were given. The International Acceptance Bank would fulfill its function by establishing a market for international bank acceptances and would then pass out of existence.

Upper Providence Harbor about 1919

In June of 1922 at a meeting of the stockholders of the Trust Company an increase of ten in the number of Directors was voted, bringing the total number to forty. The action was taken as a result of the absorption of a Pawtucket bank, the Providence County Savings Bank. A branch of Hospital Trust had been opened in the banking rooms of the former Providence County Savings Bank on May 29. This absorption had required much consultation with businessmen in Pawtucket and much planning, but it was not an unusual business transaction.

However, there is a record of a most unusual transaction in this decade. The Republicans in the state suffered a sharp setback in 1922 because the workers in the mills, long unemployed, repudiated the Republican party and in 1924 the Democrats won many offices. The Republicans, however, still held the majority in the Senate. Therefore, the Democrats, in order to deny the Republicans recognition, instituted a filibuster to delay the passing of the annual appropriation bill. In this way the Democrats hoped to starve the government of the state and to make the Republican majority yield to their proposed legislation. The filibuster lasted over six months and was finally broken up by the explosion of a bromine gas bomb in the Senate Chamber. This ended the filibuster, but the Senate appropriation bill had not been passed. Certain state employees were without salaries and so in June, 1924, twenty-three banks joined in advancing $400,000 to finance the state government. In that month, at the meeting of the Directors of the Rhode Island Hospital Trust Company, it was voted that "the proper officers of this Company be and hereby are authorized to join with other banks and trust companies of this state in an agreement to provide funds for the payment of board for children placed out by the State Home and School and of salaries and wages of officers and employees of certain public institutions." Harold H. Kelly, then a Vice President and Secretary of the Trust Company, helped the Bankers Association's agent pay off the state employees in an office in the old Market Building. The share of the Rhode Island Hospital Trust Company was not to exceed $125,000. The amount finally was $123,225 and was repaid in installments, the final balance being paid on May 1, 1925.

In this decade also, three interesting trusts came to the Bank. In May, 1921, the Boy Scouts of Rhode Island became the beneficiaries of a large bequest under the will of Captain George Bucklin. His money was left in trust with the Bank for the benefit of Rhode Island Boy Scouts, part of it to be used for a new headquarters memorial building. In 1928 land around the original Camp Yawgoog would be purchased and in the fall of 1930 construction of the Bucklin

Memorial group of buildings would begin. These would be dedicated in 1931 and from then on every Scout "trained for characterful American citizenship," which was Captain Bucklin's desire, would salute Captain Bucklin's memory as he passed through the Bucklin Memorial Arch.

In 1924 the trust of Mrs. Joseph Potter came to the Bank and under it the Rhode Island Hospital received a subscription for construction and endowment of a children's hospital. Mrs. Potter's will expressed the desire that after a stated length of time the estate should be used "for the erection, furnishing and equipment of a building or a separate wing of a building . . . for the treatment, comfort and assistance in illness and convalescence of needy and unfortunate children requiring physical aid." This is, of course, known today as the Potter Memorial Building at the Rhode Island Hospital.

Also, the trust fund known as the Old Meeting House Foundation was born in the twenties for "maintenance and renovation of the fabric of the First Baptist Meeting House in Providence." The *Evening Bulletin* of June 21, 1923, reported the formation of this trust and went on: "There will be widespread gratification among the citizens of Providence over the announcement of a plan to establish a trust fund to be known as the Old Meeting House Foundation . . . The Rhode Island Hospital Trust Company has agreed to serve as Trustee of the Foundation." The fund was a benefit not only to the church and to Brown University (its Commencements are held there), but to the people of Providence. A portion of the fund was contributed by personnel in the Bank as a memorial to William A. Gamwell, Vice President of the Trust Company from 1912 to 1918, who was long associated with the Meeting House and the Bank.

The problem of space for the Trust Department now became acute. Over fifty people were employed in the department, trusts numbered 1,126, and trust assets amounted to more than $99,000,000. The department had outgrown its quarters in what is now the main banking room of the Head Office and had spread to the balcony. It was decided to proceed at once with the new annex to the building included in the original plans drawn up in 1917. It would be constructed on the lot to the west known as the Vinton estate, and the estimated cost was $1,000,000.

Mr. West pointed out at a meeting in July, 1926, the immense service which this Trust Department was rendering to the community. He reminded his listeners that the majority of people were still unaware of the type of service available to them at the Bank, and he suggested "that the Directors, because of their association and influence, could be of the greatest assistance in informing the public of the work of the Department and bringing to it (the Department) the new business which it was well organized to handle." However, many people had accepted the fact (and more would do so as time went on) that the duties of a trustee and executor called for specialized experience and that the personnel of the Trust Department had this experience; that, in fact, it was economical to turn such matters over to the department since it charged reasonable fees and was organized to take care of all the work entailed.

By 1966 there would be twelve divisions in the Trust Department; among them an Estate Planning Division headed by Daniel S. Codman, Vice President; an Agency Division under the direction of Charles B. Cornelius, Vice President; an Estates Division with Granville V. Henthorne, Vice President, in charge; an Investment Division with John W. Wall, Vice President, in charge.

In 1925 the New England Council with seventy-two members was formed. The delegates not only represented all the New England states, but also all the major industrial, commercial, and agricultural activities of the region. The council had three purposes: to stimulate concrete expressions as to matters vital to the welfare of New England, to unite action among individual states, and to promote New England industry and transportation, public utilities, and other matters of common concern. Each of the six states represented had twelve members. One of the members from Rhode Island — and a founder of the council, as well — was Henry D. Sharpe, an active Director of the Rhode Island Hospital Trust Company from 1911 to his death in 1954. Raymond H. Trott (later to be elected President of the Bank) was (and still is in 1966) active in this organization. The New England Council remains a strong force in New England business.

At the fifty-ninth Annual Meeting of the Bank the President reported that more than fifty perpetual trusts were being cared for by the Company. He reported also that the Rhode Island Foundation had had additional bequests, that there was satisfactory growth in all departments, and that the Foreign Department was still meeting the Fabre Line boats to change money for the incoming passengers.

The Trust Company had grown and was growing. It would continue to grow with the times.

CHAPTER SEVEN

World War I Memorial in Post Office Square, Lower East Side, late 1950's

1927-1936

This was boom-time in America; the day of the flapper, the Charleston, Florida real estate, and speculation on the stock market. These were the "roaring twenties."

At the meeting of the Directors of the Rhode Island Hospital Trust Company in January, 1927, sub-committees were appointed to assist the Executive Committee. To take care of the people who wished banking services in other parts of town, away from Westminster Street, it was decided to establish two branches, one at Thayer and Angell Streets to be known as the East Side Office, and one on Weybosset Street at the junction of Broad to be known as the West Side Office.

In May, Lindbergh flew solo from Mineola, Long Island, to Paris and because air travel was obviously going to be permanent, the word "Providence" in letters 20 feet high was painted twice on the roof of the Trust Company's Head Office in the fall, each word being 140 feet long and visible from an airplane 2,000 feet in the air. It had been requested by the United States Department of Commerce "that all cities be marked for the benefit of aviators who may have lost their bearings" and the Trust Company responded to the request. It would be over thirty years (in 1959) before any other sign would be put on the Head Office and then it would take six months of persuasion by the President of the Bank to have it done.

That spring of 1927 a design was chosen for a World War I memorial in Post Office Square; the new Brown Gymnasium was under construction, as was the new wing of the Bank. This annex, to house the Trust Department, was finished late in the year and that department moved in in December. Twenty phones were installed in the new wing. The very fact that the Trust Department had grown enough to warrant this move to larger quarters proved that the founders of the Bank had "uncanny powers of prognostication in anticipating the national trend toward the corporate fiduciary," for in the beginning the trust business had been so unfamiliar to the public that a trust company seemed an anomaly.

The Foreign Department had grown, too. In October, 1927, it reported that the volume of business handled had increased over $15,000,000 in the preceding fiscal year. This department would not be able to report gains during the thirties because of the Depression, nor in the early forties because World War II would curtail travel and the exchange restrictions of practically every country in the world would be so severe it would be almost impossible to do any foreign business. In the late forties, the fifties, and the sixties, however, its potential would be realized.

On February 8, 1928, the *Providence Journal* reported that Dr. W. H. P. Faunce had been the speaker the night before at the dinner celebrating the sixtieth anniversary of Hospital Trust. "He praised the banking profession," the newspaper account read, "as one which served the common weal by bringing together persons who need to be brought together. 'You serve the admirable purpose,' he said, 'of bringing together the House of Have with the House of Want.' " About 350 persons attended — Directors, officers, and employees — and enjoyed dancing in the large banking room after dinner. Announcements of the anniversary were sent out: "To our many customers and friends who by their patronage and good will have made possible our growth and development we extend our appreciative greetings and best wishes for happiness and prosperity for many years to come." An enclosure went out with the announcement: "We are pleased to announce the completion of the Hospital Trust Building and the occupancy of the addition to our Banking Rooms by our Trust Department. You are cordially invited to call and inspect the enlarged banking quarters and the improved arrangement of our various departments."

That anniversary year Mr. West, the President, appointed Fred B. Barrows head of the Statistical Department. For almost a decade, while he was statistician, Mr. Barrows wrote a weekly column for the *Providence Journal*. He progressed, over a period of thirty-five years, from credit analyst to bank economist. When he was about to retire in 1960, he said, "They paid me well for just what I love to do anyway." Within a few years of his retirement, the functions of his department would be performed by the Investment Research Division of the Trust Department.

In the last month of the year it was announced that the National Globe and Mechanics Savings Bank of Woonsocket would consolidate with the Woonsocket Office of the Rhode Island Hospital Trust Company. Other banks in this area that were part of the Trust Company were the Producers National, absorbed in 1925, and the Producers Savings, absorbed in 1926. Many of these absorptions, and others before and afterward, were supervised by Ralph W. Bowen, Vice President of the Trust Company, who, in 1966, is an Honorary Director and a member of the Pawtucket Board of Managers of the Trust Company.

In the same month, at the Annual Meeting of the stockholders, the President reported that 1928 had been an unusual year, that interest rates were low and that deposits were high in the beginning but reversed later in the year

Col. Lindbergh's plane "Spirit of St. Louis" at Quonset — 1927

so that interest rates stiffened, which caused all deposits to decline. He also reported that surplus deposits were withdrawn in many cases. Yet there was exceptional prosperity. The metal trades especially were operating at a record-breaking pace. The capital stock of the Company was increased from $3,000,000 to $4,000,000.

Ten months later, in October, 1929, the picture changed. Stocks declined all over the world and in November came the stock market crash. An editorial of the day stated:

The collapse must be looked upon as the inevitable aftermath of a prolonged period of excessive speculation. The stock market has for months been front page news; its demands for funds have drawn gold and credit from all corners of the globe and raised the world-level of its interest rates. Tightening money rates have restricted building construction, hampered foreign trade and placed a burden on all business activity. The vast amount of liquidation that has just occurred has released credit, has already brought lower money rates and should ultimately better business in general, particularly those forms of business requiring bond and mortgage financing. The Federal Reserve System, the strongest banking organization in the world, is in excellent condition to supply the necessary credit to business now that the speculative mania has been cured.

The President of the Bank reported later that "the banks were in a strong position, money rates continued to drop and the purchasing power of wage earners was apparently unaffected for some months." By the middle of 1930, however, business began to be affected so that by the end of that year the American people were in the midst of the severest business depression since the Civil War. The banking situation was somewhat better in Rhode Island than elsewhere, but the cotton textile business, which was a staple of the state, locally was worse than in the country as a whole. There was a decrease of 47 per cent of the consumption of cotton in Rhode Island as against 25 per cent nationally. By November acute pressure forced sixty-two banks in various states to close their doors, and a year after the crash unemployed men were selling apples on the streets of Providence under the auspices of the Providence Unemployment Committee.

And yet there were light moments, too. For instance, in January, 1931, the Rhode Island Hospital Trust Company decided to wage war against the starlings on the ledges of the building. Steeplejacks climbed the Exchange Place side of the building and routed ten thousand starlings by circling the building on the ledge and then on the roof and shooting off thirty-six hundred Roman candles. There was another offensive the next month but only temporary relief was obtained.

In his Annual Report for 1931, the President reported that business activity was still at the depressed level to which it had fallen in 1930. Employment was 20 per cent below normal. It was the worst depression in half a century. A revival by textiles in the spring proved short-lived and was followed by a decline in building activity and real estate turnover. Mr. West reported:

The banking situation which has been such a disturbing factor in many parts of the country has remained sound in Rhode Island. In only three other states and the District of Columbia have there been no bank failures in the first ten months of this year. During that period there were 1,753 bank suspensions for the country as a whole involving a total of $1,461,852,000 in deposits. As a consequence of the large number of bank failures, the practice of hoarding currency increased alarmingly during the Summer and Fall, but it has not been prevalent in New England and for the nation as a whole appears now to be on the wane.

The new position of Comptroller was created in 1930. Only two men have held this title in the almost four decades since: Oscar T. Sherman, from 1930 to 1950, and Harold W. Thomas, who assumed this position in 1950 and still holds it today. Mr. Thomas is also a Vice President.

Mr. West had been an untiring worker for the city and state during this time and recognition was given him by the President of the United States. A newspaper account read:

Not only Providence but the entire state was honored during the past week when Thomas H. West, Jr., President of the Rhode Island Hospital Trust Company and chairman of the Providence Unemployment Committee, was appointed a member of a national committee of 19 welfare leaders to administer unemployment relief next winter and also representative for Rhode Island of the President's Organization's Committee on Administration of Relief. He has directed various welfare projects and is Chairman of the Providence Emergency Unemployment Committee which during 1931 has raised and administered a fund of almost $6,000,000.

In accord with the depressed state of business the first dividend in many years for less than 4 per cent per annum on savings accounts was declared in 1932. Notice had been given to the depositors that the reduction would be made. It is interesting to note that withdrawals were less that year of 1932 than they were six months earlier for a similar period. At the end of 1932 salaries of officers and other employees would be reduced as part of the retrenching program.

In April, 1932, Pawtucket underwent a financial crisis and established a line of credit with three banks for enough money to meet payrolls and other obligations until tax-time in the fall. The credit was contingent on the sale of a $1,200,000 serial bond issue and the sale of $1,680,000 of construction bonds to outside brokers and banks. The Rhode Island Hospital Trust Company agreed to buy $1,000,000 worth of tax anticipation notes. Other banks around Rhode Island also helped by purchases.

Exchange Place (now Kennedy Plaza) and trolley cars, mid 1920's

The number of bank failures in the United States now rose to thirty-five hundred. All banks everywhere felt the impact of business bankruptcies and the shrinkage of bond prices. As a direct result, the Rimnik Corporation was formed at the Bank in 1932 to hold title to foreclosed and acquired real estate in the Midwest (Rimnik stood for Rhode Island, Minnesota, Nebraska, Iowa, and Kansas). When New England industry began to pick up and there was a demand for money in the East, the corporation was dissolved.

The President of the Rhode Island Hospital Trust Company in his Annual Report for 1933 said,

during the closing months of 1932 and the first quarter of 1933, political uncertainty and later the financial panic which led to the complete suspension of banking activities throughout the country brought about a steady decline in industrial activity which reached its low point in March when it was 47% below normal ... The most dramatic incident in the financial world during the past year was the so-called Bank Holiday starting on March 4 and ending March 14 and 15. During those 10 days when all normal banking operations were suspended, every effort was made by the banks in Rhode Island to cooperate as far as they were permitted by law to keep business from absolute stagnation. Rhode Island was one of the few states and perhaps the only one that issued scrip in order to keep business alive. New enabling acts had to be drawn and passed by the Legislature in order to legalize the issuance of this makeshift money which temporarily relieved the situation. Finally on March 14 the Providence banks received their licenses to reopen and on the following day all of the banks in the state ... with one exception were open and doing business.

Rhode Island was the only state in the Union without a bank failure just before the Bank Holiday, and the story of that Holiday as it concerned the Rhode Island Hospital Trust Company in Providence is interesting. Mr. West was called by a Boston banker at 4:30 A.M. on March 4, 1933. He in turn called Lieutenant Governor Robert E. Quinn, Acting Governor in the absence of Governor Theodore Francis Green (who was in Washington for the inauguration of Franklin Delano Roosevelt), and other bankers in the city and asked them to come to his home at 2 George Street as soon as possible. There was a great sense of urgency because an announcement had to be made in the newspapers which were then about to go to press. At 5:45 A.M. Acting Governor Quinn proclaimed a one-day banking moratorium for Rhode Island for March 4 at the request of leading bankers (the last Bank Holiday was Armistice Day, 1918). A bankers' committee was appointed consisting of the clearing house committee and others to represent all the banks in the state. On Monday, March 6, money-changing bureaus were opened at 69 Mathewson Street and in the Town Hall, East Greenwich, to relieve the merchants of embarrassment when they could not make change. A vault at Providence Police Headquarters and one at a state police barracks were opened to merchants for the deposit of large sums. That same day a measure was drawn up by Acting Governor Quinn providing for the issuance of scrip to serve as a medium of exchange while the banks were closed. Acting Governor Quinn said, "Have confidence and faith in Franklin D. Roosevelt and he will lead the American people out of the chaos and demoralization into which we have fallen to a new deal, a higher plane of culture and living, to a nobler, happier and finer life." President Roosevelt's proclamation had declared the Bank Holiday, March 6 to 9 inclusive. On Tuesday, safe deposit boxes were made available to owners in Rhode Island and much cash was released from them. On that day, too, the scrip was ready. It measured three by seven inches, was tinted, and numbered by series. The tint on the back was the same on all denominations, while on the face it varied with the denomination. The tints, we are told in a book published about the Bank Holiday, "were colors which were extremely difficult to duplicate by any method." What these colors were was never divulged. A total of $8,510,000 in scrip was printed under special guard with the cooperation of all the banks, the Providence Police Department, and the Rhode Island State Police. From Sunday, March 5, at 10:00 P.M., to Saturday, March 11, at 4:30 A.M., the J. C. Hall Company, which printed the money, was in operation on the scrip for a total of 121 hours out of a possible 126½ hours. Bank employees were on duty there and also men from the Providence Clearing House.

On March 8 a bill was passed to speed the opening of Rhode Island banks and the *News-Tribune* in Providence reported that the

Rhode Island banking situation is being solved in the open . . . On a broad and softly carpeted dais at the southern end of the banking rooms of the Rhode Island Hospital Trust Company the best minds of the Rhode Island banking community are concentrated in great numbers . . . In this space usually devoted to the functioning of the bank officers, bankers are almost stepping on one another's toes as they move purposefully from conference to conference. . . . There is an air around those conferences of concentrated banking knowledge, of a tremendous amount of practical information, bent to the sole end of solving a practical and pressing problem.

Some banks opened on a limited basis on March 8 and two days later all banks opened. However, Governor Green limited the amount of scrip distribution; he made ten dollars a week available to each person. On the day the banks opened hoarders brought back their gold. On the thirteenth of March, eight Reserve member banks in Providence fully reopened and two commercial banks were also opened. On the fourteenth, ten commercial banks resumed

G. Burton Hibbert
President 1936-1947

business on an unrestricted basis. All scrip was to be turned in by May 15, but on that date there was still $5,500 outstanding. On the whole Providence banks acquitted themselves well in the crisis of 1933; only one in the state did not reopen. "As a result, the general confidence of the public remained good and there [was] a minimum of ill will to live down."

The emergency was over and the officers and Directors of the Bank could now turn their attention to another matter. The first hint of this — a change in the life of the Trust Company — had come in April when Mr. West reported that a great deal of pending legislation "might compel this Company to become a national bank, as all banks might be forced into one system under Government control." This referred to the Banking Act of the next year (1934) separating security affiliates from commercial banks, establishing the Federal Deposit Insurance Corporation, prohibiting interest on demand deposits, and permitting statewide branch banking for national banks where allowed by state bank laws among other new restrictions and revisions. He also touched on the possibility that the Trust Company might be compelled to divorce its Trust Department from the Commercial Banking Department. In August, at the meeting of the Board of Directors, the President explained the national code as it was expected to apply to the banks and also the bankers' modification which had been approved by President Roosevelt.

At a special meeting of the Board of Directors on November 29, 1933, it was voted to recommend to the stockholders the formation of a national bank to be known as the Rhode Island Hospital National Bank. It was in the interest of sound banking to bring about the separation of the strictly commercial business from the trust and savings business. As a result, on November 29, the following letter was sent to depositors of the Rhode Island Hospital Trust Company:

To Our Depositors:

At a special meeting of the Board of Directors held today, it was voted to recommend to the stockholders the formation of a national bank to be known as the Rhode Island Hospital National Bank and to be wholly owned by the Hospital Trust Company with the exception of Directors' qualifying shares. The new bank would have a capital and surplus of five million dollars and would take over all the commercial and foreign business now conducted by the Trust Company. As a national bank, it would be automatically a member of the Federal Reserve System. The plan has been worked out after consultation with officials of the Federal Reserve Bank, the Federal Reserve Board, the Department of the Comptroller of the Currency and the Bank Commissioner of Rhode Island. As stated in a letter mailed to the Trust Company's stockholders today, this separation of the commercial from the other departments conforms to the policy that a more centralized consolidated banking system is not only desirable, but inevitable; that the separation of our commercial business and making it a full-fledged part of the national system is a logical step toward that end; that the Trust and Savings functions are distinctly local ones best conducted under state laws ... If the plan goes into effect, it is expected that the new bank will start business on January 2, 1934.

The stockholders voted in December at the Annual Meeting to create a bank to handle their commercial business. The National Bank became a member of the Federal Reserve System, and the Trust Company retired from the Federal Reserve System and discontinued its commercial banking business.

During the planning for the separation Herbert J. Wells died. He had been President of Hospital Trust for thirty-five years, Chairman of the Board for fourteen. A minute was spread on the record. It read:

The passing of Herbert Johnson Wells, who died at his home in Kingston, October 27, 1933, removes from the Board of Directors of this Company its oldest member in point of service, and for 14 years past, its Chairman. Previous to assuming this position he served for a full generation as President of this Company. Born in Wakefield, Rhode Island, July 13, 1850, of a line of country bankers, receiving a lengthy experience in banking in a neighboring institution, he became connected with the Rhode Island Hospital Trust Company in 1881 as Secretary; on December 4, 1883, he was elected Vice President; and the following June 16, 1884, became President, this last election being supplemented by that of Director on December 1, 1885. As President of the Company, he served for over 35 years, until October 31, 1919, when elected to the position lately held. He thus completed over 52 years of official connection with the Company.

No banker of his generation more impressed himself upon an institution than did Mr. Wells as President of this Company. Throughout the years he built up the personnel with rigid standards as to character, keeping track of its performance with meticulous care. To every one of the staff he was a friendly critic, interested in his success. A master of the technique of banking operation, his energy permeated every department of the organization. He attracted customers by offers of progressive service, by enlarging facilities for doing modern business, as well as by his personal interest in their welfare. Under his guidance the trust business not only flourished to a remarkable degree, but became a distinguishing feature of local banking service. Aside from leadership in this institution, he gave leadership to banking in his city and state. In every association among banks, in any movement for the upholding of the banking profession, in the adjustment of difficult situations in credit, in times of real financial difficulty, his experience, his forcefulness, and his character were of commanding importance ... He saw [the Bank's] resources increase ... from approximately eight million dollars to about 66 million dollars, which latter figure mounted still further during his less active years as Chairman of the Board. He actively directed an expanding accommodation of its needs, leading to a new building in 1891 ... a very considerable enlargement of this new building in 1903 and the substitution of the present very ample building ... The vision embodied in these several enlargements had his enthusiastic advocacy and guidance.

He gave unsparingly of his time and counsel to social welfare and civic and religious matters of importance ...

Mr. Wells in his character, in his integrity of opinion, and in his breadth of interest of the good of his fellow men was illustrative of the best that has endured in New England. In his going the Company has lost an old and revered servant, whose conspicuous service cannot soon be forgotten.

One other important event occurred at the end of 1934. At the Annual Meeting an amendment to the by-laws was proposed and passed that "there shall be a meeting of the stockholders annually on the fourth Tuesday of January beginning with the year 1936 at 11:00 in the forenoon at the office of the Company in Providence, Rhode Island, for the election of Directors, and for such other business as may be brought before the meeting." The Annual Meeting had until then been held on the first Tuesday in December. The last one to be held in December was in 1934. There was no Annual Meeting in 1935. In 1936 (fourteen months later) the switch-over was made, the Annual Meeting being held on January 28. The Annual Meeting would be held on the fourth Tuesday of January for thirty years, until 1966, when it would be changed to the third Thursday of February.

The year 1936 was Rhode Island's tercentenary and the Trust Company and the National Bank, of course, subscribed to the Tercentenary Jubilee Fund. There were commemorative half dollars (forty-five hundred were sold in six hours), Tercentenary three-cent stamps, exhibits, publications, and exercises. Governor Curley of Massachusetts presented a formal decree rescinding the Commonwealth's banishment of Roger Williams. There was a pageant and parades, and June 7 was proclaimed by Governor Green as Tercentenary Sunday, a day when the people of the state were to give thanks to Almighty God "for the full religious liberty we now enjoy due to the principle upon which the state was founded."

However, the three hundredth birthday of Rhode Island was overshadowed at the Trust Company and the National Bank by the death, in office, of Thomas H. West, Jr., on January 17, 1936. He had been President of the Rhode Island Hospital Trust Company since 1917. He was so well known in the community that his death was front-page news. He was "associated with various welfare and civic enterprises in this city," his obituary read, "and was an active worker for governmental economy. He was the guiding spirit in the raising of many millions in war bonds in this state ... He was one of the founders of the Rhode Island Community Fund and a signer of the original articles of association of the fund. . . . In 1921 he became City Chairman of the national Budget Committee formed by General Charles G. Dawes, then Director of the Budget, to promote business-like administration of governmental affairs

First Baptist Meeting House built in 1775 "for the publick Worship of Almighty God; and also for holding Commencement in." Dome of First Church of Christ Scientist (built in 1908) in background.

with a view to reducing Federal taxes." In line with this he organized a local committee known as the "Budget Guard." He played an extremely important role in Rhode Island's financial and business life as President of one of the largest banks in New England.

G. Burton Hibbert was elected President to succeed Mr. West. He had been born in Providence in 1881, and had started his career as a banker in 1900 with the First National Bank of Providence. When the Rhode Island Hospital Trust Company absorbed the First National, Mr. Hibbert continued with the Trust Company. He served as an Assistant Vice President from 1920 to 1931, was elected to the Board of Directors in 1931, and was to remain President until 1947 when he would be elected Chairman of the Board. When he received an Honorary Master of Arts Degree in 1943 from Brown University, the citation delivered by President Wriston read: "By the expenditure of time, skill and energy beyond all reasonable demands, you furnished leadership in supplying the Red Cross, the USO, Foreign Relief Agencies and our community services with financial support in full measure — heaped up, pressed down and running over. Beyond all that, your wise insight helped overcome social isolationism and fortified our common democratic faith. In recognition of these and your many other achievements, I welcome you to this company (Brown) with admiration and affection."

To serve with Mr. Hibbert, William S. Innis was elected First Vice President. This designation was not in reference to the fact that he was the senior Vice President; it referred to a new office, today called Executive Vice President. Mr. Innis would remain First Vice President until his death in 1943.

During Mr. Hibbert's first year in office there were many department changes and relocations in an effort to centralize the National Bank departments on the east side of the main lobby and the Real Estate and Mortgage Departments of the Trust Company on the west side.

The year 1936 was the best for Rhode Island business since 1930. The sharp upward trend in cotton textiles in the fall was the outstanding industrial event in Rhode Island that year.

An article in *Banking* a few years earlier stated that the Rhode Island Hospital Trust Company "Throughout its history . . . has been quick to adopt new methods that at the same time are safe and conservative. Up until the new building was well under way, it was not a great user of advertising. With the completion of the building it began to use larger newspaper space than any other bank in the city, to publish and distribute booklets regarding its activities and to use letters liberally for the purpose of building up the banking business." Now radio, a new advertising medium, had been invented. It was used by the Trust Company and the National Bank for the first time in November when they participated with forty other banks throughout the country in a thirty-nine-week program featuring the Philadelphia Orchestra and such nationally known speakers on finance as Willard M. Kiplinger and Walter R. Pitkin.

Rhode Island's tercentenary year was drawing to a close but the year ahead was also an anniversary year — the seventieth birthday of the Rhode Island Hospital Trust Company.

Tercentenary coins arrive. First shipment, three bags — one each from the Denver, San Francisco, and Philadelphia mints, is inspected by committee in Directors' Room of the Bank — 1936.

Left to right — Henry D. Sharpe, Robert F. Munro, Howard M. Chapin, Will S. Taylor, Royal B. Farnum.

CHAPTER EIGHT

Exchange Place (Kennedy Plaza) under water during the 1938 hurricane

1937-1946

The years 1929 to 1933 were the worst of the financial depression, but the federal government acted to halt deflation and in June, 1937, business began to expand again. However, the expansion did not last. G. Burton Hibbert, President of the Rhode Island Hospital Trust Company and the Rhode Island Hospital National Bank, in his Annual Report for that year, stated:

1937 witnessed the swiftest transition on record from prosperity to depression. At its beginning the prices of securities and commodities were high and rising, and business was booming. At the end commodities and stock prices were down 35 to 40 per cent respectively from their high and business was prostrated. . . . The business recovery from 1933 through 1936 was unbalanced and unsound. The recovery from earlier depressions has been automatic, self-generating and sturdy, the heavy industries having been the backbone; while in this one the emphasis has been altogether too much on light industries . . . Furthermore, that recovery was artificially stimulated. The rapid expansion of 1933 . . . was caused solely by the conviction that the NRA would greatly increase all costs and prices. There was also the stimulus of the Administration's drive to raise commodity prices to the 1926 level. Then came the various governmental devices for "priming the pump" with the climax coming in the middle of 1936 with the distribution of $2,700,000,000 largely the bonus . . . Most people agree that the major handicap to business recovery is lack of confidence.

Not because of worsening business conditions, but because it seemed the proper time, a new committee was formed in the Trust Department on February 1, 1938, to be known as the Industries Committee of the Rhode Island Hospital Trust Company. It was a subcommittee of the Trust Committee, and its function, according to the minutes of the meetings held, was to be "primarily concerned with those companies in which our trust interest is substantial, particularly those companies with relatively inactive markets for their securities." The committee reviewed the current and past operating performances of the companies concerned, their financial condition, their dividend record, and their managerial problems. One report of this committee states: "attending meetings are those members of Trust and Banking Departments who are considered best qualified to contribute to the work of the Committee. Also, there are invited to individual meetings the officers primarily responsible for the accounts holding the stocks under discussion and representatives of the management of the companies, particularly where a controlling interest is owned." (In 1966 Philip B. Simonds, Co-Vice President in charge of the Trust Department with Frederick E. Atkinson, is chairman of the Industries Committee. Mr. Simonds and Mr. Atkinson have both had long careers in the Trust Company. Mr. Simonds came to Hospital Trust in 1929; Mr. Atkinson in 1918. Mr. Simonds became a Trust Officer in 1948; Mr. Atkinson in 1944. They became co-officers in charge of the Trust Department in 1959.)

In the spring of 1938 a greater menace than a recession came into view on the world horizon. Adolf Hitler took direct charge of the German army and joined Austria to Germany, defying the world in an address at Linz.

Concern with the threat of war was temporarily blown out of Rhode Islanders' minds by the hurricane and tidal wave of Wednesday, September 21, 1938. Afterwards, a book called *The Hurricane and Flood of September 21, 1938, As They Affected the Rhode Island Hospital Trust Company* was written by John H. Wells, Vice President of the Company from 1919 to 1951. He was a son of Herbert J. Wells. From 1939 to 1951 he would be in charge of the Savings Department. He had created what had become the Public Relations Department and the Central Files Department, and he was instrumental in organizing the Advertising Department.

The water, we are told by Mr. Wells, began to come into the building about 5:15 P.M. The Trust Company was built on the so-called water lots and, when the tide rose, the Head Office was more vulnerable than almost any other piece of property in the city. In those days there were basement windows in the building and these broke with the force of the wind and the water. The velocity of the water coursing through the lobby of the building was nearly ten miles per hour. "The water rushing through the arcade, forcing its way under and around the doors to the Bank and Trust Departments and rushing down elevator wells and stairways to the basement made a roar which, to say the least, was terrifying and ominous."

As an aside, one must remember that when the first building on Westminster Street was renovated, it was proposed that the Safe Deposit Department "be a very elaborate system of vaults . . . to be carefully protected above and below from water." The new building of 1917 was also carefully constructed but no planning could foresee tidal waves. At 7:45 P.M. on the day of the hurricane, after the tide changed, Mr. Hibbert, the President, returned to the building. Harold J. Field (then Assistant Trust Officer) had gone to escort him downtown. Mr. Hibbert was advised to wear rubber boots, the first mention of an item that was to become extremely common in the days ahead. At 9:30 P.M. there was a conference of officers at which time it was decided that the water must be pumped out of the basement quickly. Thursday morning fire pumps were working there. Looters were on the prowl downtown, but also walking the streets were members of the National Guard, mobilized to protect private property. The National Bank and the Trust Company opened Friday for payrolls. There were no rugs or furniture in the Banking or Trust Departments (all were at the cleaners); vaults in the Safe Deposit Department were still being pumped. The customers' vault was opened on Friday, but only a few people were allowed to go down to drain their boxes. On Saturday chairs were set in rows near the exhibition case in the lobby and people waited there for their turn to go downstairs. The coupon rooms were not usable and so caterers' tables and chairs were placed around the vault while as many as 125 laborers and 100 mechanics worked in the vault simultaneously. Employees of the Trust Company and the National Bank wore boots all the time (there were more boots at that location than since 1867, the year the Company was founded, when A. C. Eddy sold hip, knee, and short boots wholesale and retail at 15 Westminster Street). Although there was extensive general damage, the building was not structurally impaired. Radio hams operated a radio to the East Side Office which had a working telephone. All the telephones downtown were out of order. And yet, on the following Monday the National Bank and the Trust Company were able to open their doors to the public without restriction. A meeting of the Clearing House banks had been held on Saturday and it was decided then that the clearing would be made in the office of the Bank, which also offered cash and coin to the other banks if they needed it.

Blotters — sixty-two reams of them, or thirty-one thousand — we are told by Mr. Wells, were used for drying out safe deposit boxes in the wet area of the vault; the water had been almost three feet high there. Oil stoves and flatirons were used for drying securities, also photostat-drying machines, electric mangles, and Pantex pressing machines operated by kerosene with vents projecting from basement windows on Washington Row. The Purchasing Department kept up with the demand for rubber boots, flashlights, cheesecloth, vaseline and steel wool (for vault doors), disinfectant, kerosene, wool socks (to ease sore feet), tables and chairs, bottled water, fire extinguishers, and sandwiches and coffee twice a day for at least two hundred people.

Notices were sent to all safe deposit box holders on September 26 asking them to come in to drain their boxes, but a week after the vault was opened some boxes had not been attended to and water was seeping out of them. On September 30 it was decided to drill holes in these wet boxes and pour off the water. Registered letters were sent to all holders of such boxes. Five persons attended each drilling (two Bank officers, a representative of counsel, a York safe man to drill, and a vault attendant to seal). The box was held unopened over a pail covered with cheesecloth, to catch any small object that might fall through the hole, and the water poured out. The box was then wound with wire, given an identification tag, and the ends of the wire sealed. A certificate was signed by a team of three officials. Three hundred and seventy-one boxes were drilled in this way until the owners came in to secure new ones.

The Safe Deposit Department bore the brunt of the damage and everyone worked down there. Mr. Hibbert, the President, for instance, did not sit at his own desk until 11:50 A.M., Wednesday, September 28, a week after the hurricane.

The Disaster Loan Corporation, part of the Federal Housing Administration, a federal agency, was established in Providence on September 28, 1938. The Corporation was to make loans for repairs and rehabilitation and the Bank

Pumping hurricane water from Bank

Drying out securities with "Pants Presser"

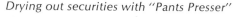

applied to it for a license to make loans on property damaged by the hurricane and flood. After the license was received, this work was carried on in the Loan Department.

Many incidents made good copy for newspapers around the country. One reported, "Watered Stock Is Sent to Cleaners; Guess the Result." Another told the story of an old lady who accepted the offer to take her safe deposit box home to dry out the contents. Armored cars and State Police were available as escorts in such cases. The old lady was sent home in a taxi with State Police accompanying it, sirens screaming. "Never enjoyed a ride so much in my life," she said. When she got home she opened her box and hung the damp papers on a clothesline outside her back window. "I felt rather furtive about it," she added, "after they had taken all that trouble."

Frederic J. Hunt, Trust Officer at that time, has recalled that not a security was lost and that most of the bonds came through without any blurring of the ink. There was one exception: municipal bonds of the early twenties. The ink on those ran and the state legislature had to give authority to validate them. The reason that these particular issues of bonds were damaged was that prior to the war dyestuffs usually came from Germany. In 1920, just after the war, the United States was no longer importing German chemicals but had not yet developed any of comparable quality.

As an aftermath of the hurricane, the sidewalk (basement) windows were filled in with granite and the west wall was rebuilt. Plans were made to fix the entrances to the building so they would be watertight. The repairs after the tidal wave and hurricane cost $259,847.31, but some of this was recoverable from insurance. The watermark of this hurricane was higher than that of the Great Gale of 1815; two plates on the building attest to this. Destroyed after the hurricane because they were submerged and because the expense of drying them out was disproportionate to their value, were old letter books, auditors' books, correspondence of Herbert J. Wells, canceled checks, Banking and Trust Department letters for 1920 to 1924, old stock registers, old salary receipts, old dividend records, and many more items.

The minutes of the October meeting of the Board of Directors read: "The Board of Directors of the Rhode Island Hospital Trust Company hereby records its high appreciation of services performed by the officers, staff and employees following the hurricane and its resulting tidal flood which occurred on the evening of Wednesday, September 21 — an event unparalleled in the history of the community. . . . Every credit is accorded to the admirable leadership of the President and his immediate staff and to the superb cooperation of everyone of the force of the Company all of whom exhibited team play of a distinguished character."

The subject of the hurricane would recur from time to time until December, 1939, when, at the Annual Meeting, an itemized list would be presented of repairs, renovations, and additions made to the building. The vault and basement repairs would not be completed until June, 1939.

Statewide the damage was set at 100 million dollars by Governor Quinn. Martial law prevailed in many sections into October. The death toll was finally set at 258 in Rhode Island with fourteen missing.

News of the hurricane was finally removed from the front page of the newspapers and was replaced by the report of military events in Europe. In 1939 Germany invaded Poland. In May and June, 1940, in a five-week period, Holland was vanquished by the Nazis, Belgium capitulated, and France surrendered — the ninth European country to fall under Nazi control since Hitler had taken Austria. The shock of the Nazi blows was reflected in markets everywhere and precipitated the heaviest gold movement in history. War was imminent and the state of Rhode Island would be an important place during World War II with Quonset, Davisville, Melville, and the Newport Naval Base all located here.

Rhode Island business seemed to be running ahead of the rest of the country in 1941. This was due to the fact that it was a center for the machine-tools industry and also for the cotton and woolen industries. Another reason for its high employment rate was the location of the Northeastern Naval Air Base at Quonset Point. This was commissioned in July, 1941, and was the largest naval air base on the North American coast.

During the first year of the war two Directors, five officers, and forty-one employees joined the armed services. The skylights in the National Bank and Trust Company building were removed and replaced by nonshatterable material and an air-raid shelter was arranged in the basement. A loudspeaker system was installed over which instructions could be given during practice or actual air raids. Vital bank records were duplicated, each set to be stored in a different place. Trucks were made available to transfer the records to other vaults at the first sound of an alert. An interesting sidelight of the war news was that Florence T. Newsome, the first WAC to enlist from Rhode Island, was a receptionist of the Rhode Island Hospital Trust Company. She became a Lieutenant Colonel (one of the first to be appointed) and later served on General Marshall's staff.

Mr. Hibbert in his Annual Report to the stockholders on January 27, 1942, talked about the war: "The increased burdens placed upon those who

Quonset Point before Naval construction

Present Naval Air Base at Quonset Point, commissioned 1941

have remained have been accepted without question," he said, "and with a sense of loyalty not only to their country, but to this Company. They have spared no effort to maintain the Bank's standards of service to the public and I wish here to make an acknowledgment of that fact." He re-emphasized his recommendation of the year before that Defense Bonds must be sold in increased amounts and that individuals should invest all current savings in those bonds. "There is every good reason why this debt should be held by the public," he explained, "and not by the banks. It should become a part of our permanent money supply." He reported higher earnings for the Trust Company and broad gains in Rhode Island business. The combined earnings of the Trust Company and National Bank were $1,170,513 compared to the previous year's total of $929,163. He said that the trust business continued to be satisfactory.

The following fall at a meeting of the Board of Directors Mr. Hibbert read a memorandum: "Before we assemble again this Company will have passed its 75th milestone. It was on October 24, 1867, that it was officially founded; for on that date the original incorporators met after having obtained the required minimum stock subscription aggregating $200,000; elected a Board of Directors and President; appointed a committee to prepare by-laws; and adjourned. The meeting was held close to this spot in the Horse Guards' Armory at 11 Westminster Street." Because the seventy-fifth anniversary came during a war, no celebration marked its passing.

In 1942 the Foreign Department took subscriptions for Series E, F, and G War Bonds and Tax Notes and a booth for selling bonds was erected in the center of the Head Office. This wartime activity was added to the usual work of this department and so additional personnel had to be hired. The war work was not confined to the Foreign Department; it spread through the entire organization and involved extra work in all departments. It was the story of World War I all over again, even to the campaigns to raise money. During World War II the Community Chests and the War Fund campaigns were merged into the United War Fund and this organization was directed for a time by Mr. Hibbert. William S. Innis, First Vice President, also served as a director of the United War Fund. When he died in 1943, his obituary referred to him not only as a banker, but as a banker-philanthropist.

By the spring of 1943 the Real Estate and Mortgage Departments were forced to move elsewhere and their offices were occupied by the War Activities Department. Payroll checks were cashed there, subscriptions to all issues of War Bonds were made there, ration banking was conducted there, and withholding taxes would be paid there (this tax on all salaries would become effective July 1, 1943).

The war continued to take time and men. By 1944 three Directors, six officers, and forty-four employees had enlisted or were drafted into the services. Female employees now outnumbered males for the first time, 228 to 171. Secretary of the United States Treasury Morgenthau chose G. Burton Hibbert to lead the Third War Loan Drive and when the Treasury Department announced the organization of a new War Finance Committee for Rhode Island — to take over war financing for the state — Mr. Hibbert was named chairman.

The year the war ended, the Installment Loan Department, which had been functioning in the Mortgage Department, was set up as a separate unit with one officer and four clerks. It had started as a Personal Loan Service in 1934 with the administration of federal home loans and had grown to include auto loans and income tax financing among other services. The Installment Loan Department was mainly the idea of Lincoln E. Barber, Vice President from 1936 to his death in 1951. In 1966 there are four officers and forty-nine clerks in the department.

An interesting subject was discussed at the next Annual Meeting in January, 1945; a recommendation to the stockholders in connection with a donation to the Rhode Island Hospital Building Fund. The President reviewed the history of the relations between the Hospital and the Trust Company, recalling that the Company's original charter had stipulated that a certain portion of its earnings were to go to the Hospital. He told how the Trust Company in 1880 had issued a block of stock to the Hospital and, therefore, caused the earlier provision to be canceled. Now, he said, because of this history of the two institutions and "having in mind also not only the close business relations ... but also the obligations of this Company to the community," the Executive Committee (the committee with the responsibility for administration and loans) and the Board of Directors recommended to the stockholders a subscription to the Rhode Island Hospital of $35,000. This was in the continuing tradition of the Trust Company and the National Bank; always prepared to recognize their obligation to the community.

In November of the same year the capital stock of the Trust Company, $5,000,000, consisted of 5,000 shares at $1,000 each. It was resolved (and the resolution passed) to divide it into 100,000 shares at $50.00 each. This was to become effective on December 18, 1945, and a resolution was proposed to increase the capital stock and paid-in surplus of the Rhode Island Hospital National Bank from $2,500,000 to $5,000,000. This resolution was approved on November 20, 1945.

The next month on December 31, 1945, at twelve noon, President Truman declared the "hostilities of World War II closed," although May 8 had been Victory-in-Europe Day and Japan had surrendered on August 14.

As if to start fresh after the war, the Head Office building was washed in 1946. Reviewing that year in his last report as President, Mr. Hibbert noted that the net operating earnings of the Trust Company amounted to $1,445,609 and of the National Bank to $647,046. He also noted that there were six branches in operation in 1946.

At the Annual Meeting in 1947 Mr. Hibbert was elected Chairman of the Board after having served as President for eleven years and in other capacities for thirty-six years. The new decade began with a new President — Raymond H. Trott.

CHAPTER NINE

Lands End, Newport — Bailey's Beach at left

Raymond H. Trott had joined the staff of the Trust Company in 1919. Mr. Trott studied at the Harvard Law School and had been admitted to the bar in Maine and Massachusetts. The year after he came to Hospital Trust he was elected an Assistant Trust Officer and in quick succession Trust Officer, a Director, and a Vice President. In 1947 he became the President of a bank located in a state whose population had increased 4.4 per cent in the past seven years to 745,000 and which was that year the most highly industrialized state in the Union. By 1947 Rhode Island had a 20 per cent gain in employment over the Depression years; most of this occurred in the metal, machinery, and jewelry industries. From 1948 to 1950 there would be a recession again, but unemployment would be erased by the Korean War. Deurbanization would also continue so that the population of such Rhode Island towns as North Kingstown, Middletown, and Portsmouth would increase in the decade 1940 to 1950 by tremendous percentages: 322 per cent, 118 per cent, and 78 per cent respectively. This increase in population required thought about establishing a branch or branches of the Trust Company and the National Bank on Aquidneck Island in the near future, especially since Newport in June, 1947, was selected as one of the two permanent ports for the Atlantic Fleet. For the present, two new branches were opened in the Providence area: at 1754 Broad Street in Cranston and on Taunton Avenue in East Providence. After-hours depositories had gone into service at all offices in the spring of 1947. Also, approval was voted in November of 1948 of a bid to purchase all of the stock of the National Bank of Commerce and Trust Company of Providence.

Raymond H. Trott
President 1947-1957

Mr. Trott's first Annual Report included the resignation of Preston H. Gardner on January 28, 1947. He had been associated with the Rhode Island Hospital Trust Company for sixty-nine years; he had been Head of the Trust Department, a Vice President, a Director, and had served as Chairman of the Board from 1936 to his retirement. For two generations he had worked for the Trust Company and his influence had been great. A portrait of him hangs in the Trust Reception Room.

The absorption of the National Bank of Commerce and Trust Company was an accomplished fact by the time Mr. Trott gave his second Annual Report in 1949. This bank had been chartered in 1852 and had always been concerned primarily with commercial banking. "Acquisition of the Commerce will give us a substantial volume of new business," Mr. Trott said, "a location near the retail business center and an extremely able force of officers and employees who will be a valuable addition to our staff." It was decided to operate the National Bank of Commerce as a branch. This would make the fifth branch in Providence.

A return to competition in the field of banking as well as industry was evident in 1949. It was because of this competition and because in the forties and fifties many of the older men had died or retired that a change in the character of the Company occurred. Occasionally over the years Hospital Trust had been referred to as a "Rich Man's Bank." From the forties on that term would no longer be applicable. With an expanding economy after years of tight money during the Depression the Company now became aggressive about securing business. It wanted as customers large corporations, but not large corporations only. It wanted millionaires, but not millionaires only. In the words of one of the officers it wanted "the common man and his brother" as customers. That is why CheckMaster was introduced in 1941. That is why the Installment Loan Department was formed in 1945. That is why the Trust Company and the National Bank advertised for new business by direct mail, by radio, by newspaper, and also investigated the possibility of television (WJAR-TV had begun regularly scheduled programs in July, 1949). That is why Mr. Trott in his Annual Report for that year talked about the Public Relations Department, the personnel of which tried to attract new business and in pursuit of this made many calls on customers and potential customers. That is why more branches were established and why more absorptions occurred in the forties and fifties than in any other period. Out of twelve absorptions (to 1966) five took place in the forties and fifties. Out of twenty-four branch openings (to 1964) twelve took place in the forties and fifties.

By 1950 expanding inventories with industrial production at its peak "would create a huge demand for bank credit," as Mr. Trott told his Board of Directors. It was a time of transition from peacetime to wartime (the Korean War), and Mr. Trott pointed out that Rhode Island banks were ready "to cooperate fully in a program of industrial expansion and to furnish the needed credit to the fullest extent of their resources."

In line with the desire for new business the Trust Company and the National Bank in July, 1950, offered $90.00 a share for the 20,000 shares of the Aquidneck National Bank of Newport. This offer was accepted and the stock was acquired. The Aquidneck had a capital and surplus of over $1,000,000, and had been an active bank in Newport for many years. It had been incorporated as a state bank in 1854 and as a national bank in June, 1865. Through various absorptions the Aquidneck had roots going back to 1804, to the Rhode Island Union Bank. In those days tellers were sent to Providence to get specie and carried orders similar to this one: "You will return on Sunday or Monday in Captain Baldwin's Packet. If the ice (or anything else) should prevent his coming, you will take $5,000 of the specie by the Monday's stage and leave the remainder in the branch bank as a private deposit."

In 1926 the Aquidneck had absorbed the National Exchange Bank of Newport which had merged earlier with the Island Savings Bank. For eight years it was called the Aquidneck National Exchange Bank and Savings Company; it then became the Aquidneck National Bank of Newport. The National Exchange Bank's home on Washington Square was converted into a branch office of the Aquidneck. At the request of the federal government during World War II the Aquidneck established banking facilities at the Torpedo Station, the Government Landing, and Coddington Cove. In 1950, when the Aquidneck was absorbed by the Trust Company and the National Bank, its offices on Washington Square and on Thames Street were set up as branch offices, and its Board of Directors was designated a Board of Managers of these branch offices.

The economy of Rhode Island was naturally linked to that of the country, and when 1950 became a year of unparalleled prosperity, Rhode Island shared in it. The Securities and Exchange Commission reported that individuals in the United States saved $3,800,000,000 in liquid assets in 1950, and the Bank of America reported resources of $7,617,206,104 at the end of 1950 setting new records for capital funds, deposits, and loans.

The volume of trust accounts during the year was the largest in the history of the Trust Company and the President stated that "conservatism has made the fiduciary activity of this Company . . . successful over the years."

By the next year production increased across the country and Rhode

Island was one of two states in New England whose business population or number of business establishments exceeded in 1951 the postwar peak of 1947. This was reported by the Federal Reserve Bank of Boston. The inflationary forces diminished and Mr. Trott in his Annual Report reviewing 1951 said that

an event of outstanding importance to the fiscal welfare of this country and possibly to the whole financial world was the reassertion of the independence of the Federal Reserve authorities from Treasury domination. The Federal Reserve authorities can now exercise their true function — the stabilizing of our economy. Fiscal history has shown repeatedly that one of the most potent factors in halting inflation is the reduction of borrowing by an increase in interest rates. Artificially low interest rates encourage borrowing with resulting increase in the money supply. The lowering of the support price of government securities by the Federal Reserve authorities has of course resulted in a sharp decline in the market prices of those securities in institutional portfolios. This, however, is a small price to pay if the value of our dollar can be preserved.

In December, 1965, the Federal Reserve Board would again raise the discount rate from 4 to 4.5 per cent because of a great increase in bank loans — a threat to price stability.

The American Bankers Association's publication, *Banking,* that spring gave the Trust Company and the National Bank an award in recognition of their series of institutional advertisements, "What helps Rhode Island helps all of us." This slogan was published in newspapers throughout the state, and the basic idea was to make the public more aware of the state's advantages and so win support in the solving of its problems.

In June, 1951, the state appointed a Development Council. The council's Advisory Commission was composed of seven Rhode Island bankers, industrialists, and educators. Mr. Trott was a member of this commission. He later became chairman of it and served in this capacity for almost ten years. At first the council set up studies to determine what Rhode Island had to sell, what was wrong with the state, and what ought to be corrected. The council wanted to stop industry from moving out of Rhode Island, to attract new industry, and to encourage the development and growth of small but promising native businesses; in the words of the act creating the council: "It shall guide and accomplish a coordinated, efficient and economic development of the state." The Rhode Island Development Council would become more and more active in the years to come.

Not only was the state taking a long look at itself through the studies of the Development Council, but the Trust Company and the National Bank, too, paused in the midst of their growth to take stock. The expansion of activities after World War I had required departmentalization. Now, after World War II, it became necessary to do a job evaluation survey. The purpose of this survey was to determine the relative importance of jobs, to set up salary ranges, and to describe job changes. The survey was a tool for assisting in proper salary administration. The factors considered were the knowledge and skill, human relations, degree of judgment, and degree of responsibility each job required. This evaluation still goes on today. The performance of every employee — from the lowest level to the highest — and salaries are reviewed and evaluated throughout the year. Since it has always been the policy to promote from within if possible, this evaluation furnishes the necessary data.

Also reviewed in 1951 were the functions of the Rhode Island Hospital Trust Company and the Rhode Island Hospital National Bank and, as a result, the Trust Company absorbed its wholly owned National Bank subsidiary November 1, 1951, with the stockholders voting for the absorption at a special meeting on September 25, 1951. The Trust Company immediately became a member of the Federal Reserve System. It was felt by the officers of the Trust Company that the situation which had prevailed at the time the Rhode Island Hospital National Bank was formed (January 1, 1934) no longer existed and that one bank could be run more efficiently and give better service to its customers.

Since the absorption occurred late in 1951, 1952 was generally a year of consolidation and assimilation. In 1952 the Woonsocket Trust Company was

The Towers at Narragansett Pier

Old houses in Wickford

purchased and a second branch office was opened in Woonsocket. (In 1966 the two branches are managed by Henry R. Lee, Vice President, and have a Board of Managers similar to the Pawtucket and Newport branch offices.)

The year 1953 was a turning point in the history of banking in Rhode Island. For years many small banks throughout the state were consolidated with the Rhode Island Hospital Trust Company and its Westminster Street neighbor, the Industrial Trust Company (chartered in 1886). The proposed merger in 1953 of the Phenix National Bank with Hospital Trust, and of the Providence Union National Bank with Industrial Trust moved the *Evening Bulletin* to publish charts showing the genesis of the two largest Providence banking institutions.

The Phenix National Bank which was consolidated with the Hospital Trust was an old one in the history of the city and state. There is extant a receipt for stock issued by the Phenix Bank of Providence on November 22, 1834. Its predecessor, the Farmers and Mechanics Bank, had failed in 1829 and from its ashes rose the Phenix (appropriately named), which had a prosperous existence until absorbed by Hospital Trust. The date of the transfer to the Rhode Island Hospital Trust Company was the close of business, October 31, 1953. With the acquisition of the Phenix and its business, the Trust Company acquired an interesting piece of history. In the latter half of the nineteenth century the attention of the Directors of the Phenix had been called to two Yankee brothers on Cape Cod who were in the slaughtering business; they had great ideas but not enough capital so Phenix gave them loans and advice. Their names were Edward and Gustavus Swift. They moved to Albany and then to Chicago. Their idea had been revolutionary: to put meat-packing houses on the edge of the Great Plains where the cattle were. It worked; it affected the whole history of the country and Phenix carried Swift and Company on its books until the 1920's. A number of people came to the Trust Company from the Phenix, and in 1966 they hold important positions in the Company. Among them are Harry B. Freeman, Chairman of the Board, Clarence H. Gifford, Jr., President, Warren O. Evans, Jr., Assistant Secretary and Manager of the Advertising Department, and James E. Pennell, Manager of the Safe Deposit Department.

In spite of the fact that industrial production in the United States was at the highest level in history, Rhode Island did not share in this record-breaking prosperity. Providence, with six other New England areas, was cited as being among thirty-seven sections of greatest unemployment in the country. Mr. Trott referred to this in his Annual Report for 1953. He said that the textile depression (the number of mills in Rhode Island had been reduced to thirty by 1937) from which recovery was so slow was responsible for the great unemployment, but

123

he reported that "New England is gradually diversifying its production and there is reason for confidence in the future."

Very often, too often to mention always, deaths were reported at the Bank's meetings, for the men who had been active at the turn of the century were now very old. Almost every minute read upon the death of an officer and placed on the record referred to his unselfish service which extended far beyond the doors of the Company. Most particularly such a person was Preston H. Gardner who retired from the Trust Company in 1947 and died on October 22, 1953. At the time of his death he was an Honorary Director and had been associated with the Company for almost three-quarters of a century. The President, Mr. Trott, said: "[His] keen interest in the Trust Company and its affairs covering such a long period was a valuable asset that cannot be replaced. We shall all miss him."

On August 31, 1954, Hurricane Carol hit Rhode Island. The Head Office sustained only slight damage due to the preventive measures instituted after the 1938 hurricane. The state, however, was declared a disaster area. Twelve days later Hurricane Edna hit and the Blackstone River overflowed its banks. As a direct result of these hurricanes a so-called Sparkplug Committee was formed by bankers and businessmen in downtown Providence. Herbert C. Wells, Jr., then Trust Officer, was appointed by Mr. Trott to represent the Bank on this committee, the members of which exchanged ideas for developing the downtown area of the city. This committee would go out of existence in 1955 when the Providence Chamber of Commerce would request the formation of the Downtown Business Coordinating Council. The survey of attitudes in downtown Providence conducted by the council would result in the Downtown Master Plan which is being put into effect in 1966.

Again, in 1955, a hurricane, this one Diane, hit Rhode Island, and the torrential rains caused the worst flood of the Blackstone River in modern history. Woonsocket was ravaged, with much of the area under millions of tons of debris. Forty-five hundred mill workers were idled; destruction of private and public works drove the total of property damage to 150 million dollars. Seven feet of water covered the Social District of Woonsocket and the first approach to the Social Street Office of the Trust Company was made by rowboat. Only the walls were salvageable.

That fall, when Mr. Trott was elected President of the New England Council at its thirty-first annual conference in Boston, he spoke of what was foremost in everyone's mind. He said that flood control and flood insurance were the two issues uppermost in southern New England thinking. He warned

Hurricane Carol 1954,
scene in Market Square

against "linking flood control (in New England) with public power projects." "It would be too bad," he said, "to have flood control projects used as an excuse and a vehicle for public power for which our New England region is not suited." Providence, in 1966, would dedicate the first hurricane barrier in New England which would be for flood control only — a massive expenditure to protect downtown Providence.

Operation Big Switch at the Head Office of the Trust Company took place in 1955. This was the change-over in the accounting system of the Trust Department to a tabulating machine system. It took two years of planning and an air-conditioned room was necessary to house the equipment. This system eliminated many manual operations, simplified record-keeping and filing, and freed floor space in the Trust Department. Mr. Trott, the President, referring to the new system and the reason for it, said: "It is particularly difficult to convey simply the scope of the activities of the Trust Department. In size the accounts range from the smallest estates to those running into the millions of dollars. Some accounts stay with us a short time, others are perpetual."

The first drive-in island in the history of Rhode Island banking opened at the Trust Company's new branch office at Park and Reservoir Avenues. Two other branches were under construction, one in East Greenwich and one in Pawtucket, and these, when completed, would make a total of seventeen. There was also a limited facility at the United States Naval Training Station in Newport.

Branch offices, of course, never come into existence lightly. The primary purpose of branch banking has been explained as acquiring new, and holding existing, deposits "through the local area offices convenient to a suburban-minded people." Sometimes branches are the result of absorption of existing banks in certain locales. Sometimes a certain area is studied with the idea of starting a branch there. Such a place was East Greenwich, Rhode Island. Two years before that branch opened, a survey was made "with the object of obtaining some clues concerning the outlook for a proposed branch of the Rhode Island Hospital Trust Company there [and] the best location for such a bank if established." To this end 401 interviews were conducted in homes and 116 at commercial establishments. The minimum requirements for establishing a branch bank were an adult population of 10,000, the fact that it was a trading area, a demonstrated population growth in the area, and a mixture of industrial, commercial, and residential neighborhoods. After the survey was completed and analyzed, the Trust Company in 1955 asked the state banking authorities for permission to open a branch in East Greenwich.

Some of the reasons for deciding to go ahead with this branch were that Bostitch, Inc., proposed to relocate there and Brown & Sharpe was interested in moving there from Providence. Also Davisville (the United States Naval Construction Battalion Center) and the Quonset Point Naval Air Station were nearby. East Greenwich was the center of this area. The decision to establish the branch "was also based upon policy consideration and public relations with respect to competition." The Trust Company's application to the federal authorities stated that the request for establishing the East Greenwich branch was "primarily defensive in that we believe that we will be unable to maintain our competitive position in banking unless we locate our offices in places throughout the state where banking needs exist." This same careful surveying and consideration goes on for all new branches. Each branch, of course, has its own particular problems, but each follows the conservative, fundamental policies established at the Head Office.

In 1956 there was a general sense of well being throughout the country, but there was still a labor surplus in Rhode Island and in his final Annual Report Mr. Trott spoke of this:

The highlight of the American scene in 1956 was the continuation of the business boom to the point where the revival of inflation becomes a distinct threat. Long standing records were broken on all sides. New peaks were reached in industrial production, employment, wages, national income and consumer credit to name a few . . . For the Bank 1956 was a very satisfactory year . . . [with] earnings which enabled us to pay the largest dollar amount of dividends in our history; changes in capital structure; the opening of two promising new offices and the decision to consolidate the Phenix and Commerce Offices in the Howard Building.

The changes in capital structure mentioned by Mr. Trott were made public in September when a notice in the *Providence Journal* informed the public that the Directors of the Rhode Island Hospital Trust Company were about to recommend to the stockholders of that Company that the charter be amended to provide for an increase from $5,000,000 to $8,000,000 in the Bank's authorized capital. This was desirable, the President pointed out, to increase the shares and so provide a wide distribution of stock and a broader stockholder base, and also to increase the Bank's lending power.

The Trust Company was now almost ninety years old. For the past two years it had been stressing the theme, "What helps Rhode Island helps all of us." The fortunes of the Rhode Island Hospital Trust Company were inextricably bound up with the state in which it was located. It had confidence in Rhode Island as its expansion into almost every corner of the state showed. It had by its conservative but progressive growth earned the confidence of Rhode Islanders as shown by the business the people of the state brought to the Trust Company.

CHAPTER TEN

Freeway at junction of Routes 195 and 95

1957-1966

For the second time a new President took over the reins of office at the beginning of a new decade for the Bank. Raymond H. Trott had become President in 1947. In 1957, in the ninetieth anniversary year, Harry B. Freeman, Executive Vice President, became the seventh President of the Rhode Island Hospital Trust Company. He had been in the securities business until 1942 when he joined the Providence National Bank as Trust Officer. In 1947 he became President of the Phenix National Bank in Providence. Clarence H. Gifford, Jr., President of the Trust Company in 1966, was also at the Phenix, and the two men changed that bank from a "check cashing bank" by adding Installment Loan, Trust, and Savings Departments. In a few years, under Mr. Freeman's leadership, the assets of the Phenix climbed from $13,000,000 to $34,000,000.

Mr. Freeman was held in great esteem by his colleagues in the banking world, and the fact that he was President of the Phenix was one of the reasons the Trust Company was anxious to acquire it. He came to Hospital Trust in 1953 as Executive Vice President and remained in that position until 1957. Under his guidance as President, from 1957 to 1963, the Bank would participate actively in Rhode Island's industrial development program by providing financing to build plants under the state's 100 per cent financing program. When Mr. Freeman would become Chairman of the Board in 1963 he would tell newsmen: "My theory is that banks should be run primarily for the good of the community and second and thirdly, and I consider these about equal, for the benefit of stockholders and employees." These words were a paraphrasing of Mr. Binney's words of years before that the design of the Company was originally "to conduct all its business with reference primarily to the financial interests of the community, then of its depositors . . . then of its stockholders."

The Executive Vice President who served with Mr. Freeman from 1959 to 1962 was William W. White (Vice Chairman in 1966, one of the top four

Harry B. Freeman
President 1957-1963

positions in the Trust Company). During Mr. Freeman's last year as President, Clarence H. Gifford, Jr., served as Executive Vice President.

In his first Annual Report Mr. Freeman stated that there had been accelerated growth in the decade just past and that 1957 had been a successful year in many departments. He said, "The Public Relations and Advertising Departments through every medium of communication available to them attempted to keep the name of the Bank before the public and stress the various services we were promoting, particularly savings. Our officers called on over 2,000 customers and prospects, including many out-of-state accounts."

During the anniversary year there were several newspaper stories about the Trust Company. The *Providence Journal* mentioned that "The Rhode Island Hospital Trust Company started its banking business one flight up 90 years ago and has been climbing upward ever since." As if to bear this out the officers' penthouse dining room at the top of the Head Office was built and opened on October 14, 1957, and the cafeteria was remodeled.

Also in the anniversary year the by-laws of the Company were amended to provide for an increase in the number of Honorary Directors and to specify that they be elected from the former Boards of Managers of any branch office.

A year later a recession began and by 1958 the Apponaug Company, Rhode Island's largest textile printing and finishing plant, announced it was shutting down. All operations at the Providence plant of Nicholson File would terminate in a year's time, also. To counteract this bad news came the first progress report on the Downtown Master Plan, a scheme for revitalizing downtown Providence, sponsored by the Downtown Business Coordinating Council and the City Plan Commission. A new plan for the restoration and conservation of the historic East Side of the city was also approved. The new Howard Building was opened, and it was revealed that Providence was being considered for the site of the first mechanized post office.

The actions of the Federal Reserve System affected banks throughout the year; the first half in fighting a depression and deflation and the second half in combating inflation.

Business expanded in 1959 as the nation recovered from the effects of the 1958 recession. It was the most successful year in the Trust Company's history. The Trust Department continued its growth during the year and "at the close of 1959 it had more accounts on its books, worth more than at the end of any previous year."

In 1959 the Head Office was over forty years old and again the Bank needed more room. For this purpose the building at 49 Westminster Street would be purchased in September, 1961. New roof signs were installed on the Head Office building, each letter seven feet high and four feet wide. One sign faced the new Providence River Bridge, the other the State House. These signs could well serve as a guide to airplanes in contrast to the word "Providence" painted on the roof in 1927 which had never been visible at night. The new signs were the largest and highest in the city.

In September, 1959, Harold H. Kelly retired as Secretary and Vice President of the Rhode Island Hospital Trust Company. In a newspaper interview he was revealed as a "new-era" banker, a man who helped convince the public that a banker was not an aloof, stern man. In this interview Mr. Kelly recommended that bankers make a positive contribution to the community and stated that it was most important for bank executives to participate in community affairs because they, more than other men, had a close day-to-day relationship with the public. He also suggested that bankers take a part in municipal government because he felt that a financial background and a knowledge of business and municipal problems would make a banker an asset in the city government.

This followed the ideal of the President, Mr. Freeman, and Mr. Gifford would continue this line of thinking and of action when he would become President in 1963. At that time seminars and courses in practical politics would be held in the Trust Company "to promote among [the] employees a greater awareness of the importance of a knowledge of our state." In 1965 Mr. Gifford would originate a series of luncheons with representatives of the business, civic, educational, and governmental life of Providence. The purpose of these luncheons would be to "foster acquaintance and deepen understanding among those attending."

A trust fund going back to 1676 came to the Bank in 1960 making it the first permanent trustee under the will of Dr. John Clarke, of Newport, to serve with two individual trustees. The trustees, or assigns, were appointed for life over the years and when, in 1960, one of them became ill, the two remaining trustees petitioned the Superior Court to appoint the Rhode Island Hospital Trust Company the third and permanent trustee, and this was done. (One of the individual trustees is Wilbur Nelson, Vice President and Manager of the Newport branch offices of the Bank in 1966.) Dr. Clarke — scholar, physician, minister, statesman, and patriot — was one of the founders of the first settlement on Aquidneck and the man who secured the charter of the Colony of Rhode Island from King Charles II of England. The trust fund was to be administered by three trustees at a time. Thirty-seven individuals served as trustees over the years from the time the fund was established. Dr. Clarke specified that the income from his farms in Middletown was to be used "for the reliefe of the poor or bringing up of Children unto Learning from time to time forever." This trust, known as the Middletown Trust from the location of his farms, is said to be the oldest trust in the United States. The farms are still in existence in 1966 and are known locally as the Charity Farms since the revenue from them is still used for philanthropic purposes (scholarships, for example). In 1965 the farms were considered and rejected as a possible site for the Newport Jazz Festival.

In April, 1960, the ten thousandth trust account was opened and nearly half that number were still active. The trust business had received one great impetus at the turn of the century when the corporations set out to broaden the base of their stockholder ownership by the public sale of stock. This spurred the number of individual investors many of whom did not wish to handle their own estates and turned instead to corporate fiduciaries like Hospital Trust. The second surge of business came after World War II with the growth of profit-sharing plans. From 1956 on, more and more pension funds and profit-sharing plans had come into the Bank. This form of trust had burgeoned all over the country. In 1959 the Trust Company had taken the lead among New England banks and had offered a new free service in the area of employee profit-sharing plans which had been developed by the Bank's Trust and Data Processing Departments. The service offered showed a corporation how a profit-sharing plan would adapt to its operational structure on the basis of a study made by the Bank without obligation. If the firm then decided to adopt the plan, the Trust Department stood ready to handle the profit-sharing program's trust fund. The preliminary study provided a cost analysis, clues as to whether the plan was feasible for the company, and a reasonably accurate idea of what each employee would receive in accumulated profits at normal retirement age. By 1966 profit-sharing plans and pension funds would increase 400 per cent with no end in sight.

As a result of the rebuilding of Providence new fast highways were being constructed, and because of them the 1960 census showed a substantial migration from Providence to suburban towns. The population in the capital dropped to 206,728, but this size was evidently just right for an experiment, for in October the world's first fully automated post office was dedicated in Providence.

Automation hovered over 15 Westminster Street, too. During 1960 and 1961 the Data Processing Center at the Head Office was remodeled so that new IBM equipment could be installed. The Rhode Island Hospital Trust Company was one of the first banks in the country to have two IBM Data Processing Systems: 1401 and 1410. The Trust Company received national publicity as the first American bank to adopt the 1410 system.

In 1960 the Foreign Department experienced an unprecedented rise in the demand for international banking services and during the next year, 1961, the Bank's earnings, dividends, capital funds, and total resources were all at record levels. By 1961 a shopping mall and a parking garage were mentioned as possibilities for downtown Providence.

A new Warwick Office was under construction with two drive-in windows, and renovation of the Washington Square Office in Newport was under way with the installation there of a drive-in window, the first in the Newport area for any bank. The Wakefield Office and the Howard Building Office had been opened in 1958. More branch offices and facilities were mentioned in the 1962 Annual Report. The Trust Company applied for permission to establish an office at 593 Eddy Street, the address of the Rhode Island Hospital. This could have been called a wheel-in facility because nurses did wheel in patients. This facility was the first ever to be installed anywhere in the state in a privately operated establishment, according to the Banking Commissioner's office. It was to serve two thousand employees of the Hospital, patients, visitors, service personnel, and office help in the doctors' office building nearby. Walk-up windows were installed at some branches, too, and permission to build an auto bank was requested.

In view of the uncertain times and the possibility of almost total destruction in the event of an atomic war, space was rented at the Underground Record Protective Cooperative Trust near Stafford Springs, Connecticut, and some duplicate bank records were moved there. A $300,000 vault had been constructed there by a nonprofit organization formed by a group of financial institutions. There were private storage rooms for 220 banks or business firms. In Providence the Bank established a survival area within the old vaults at 49 Westminster Street, a building purchased in 1961. Here medical supplies, sanitation kits, and rations of food to supply five thousand people for two weeks were stored. Also located in this building was the Installment Loan Department, which had doubled its business in the last six years. By 1965 the Advertising, Purchasing, Central Files, Savings Bookkeeping, and Systems and Procedures Departments would be located in this building.

Records of the Trust Company indicated that earnings and dividends, deposits, loans, and total resources were again at new highs in 1961. To provide for its expansion, the old building next to the Main Street Office, one of the

Pawtucket branch offices, was purchased in 1961. The Main Street Office was then forty years old and had a staff of fifty. (George W. Ellinwood is Vice President and Manager in 1966 of the Pawtucket branch offices.) The Warwick Office was opened in June of 1961. In Newport all kinds of events spurred business: the permanent establishment there of the Officers Candidate School, the America's Cup Races, and the redevelopment of the downtown district. The Naval Facility there served the summer White House staff, Secret Servicemen, State Department representatives, the foreign officers quartered at the Naval War College, and military personnel of all kinds.

Recent air view of Rhode Island Hospital

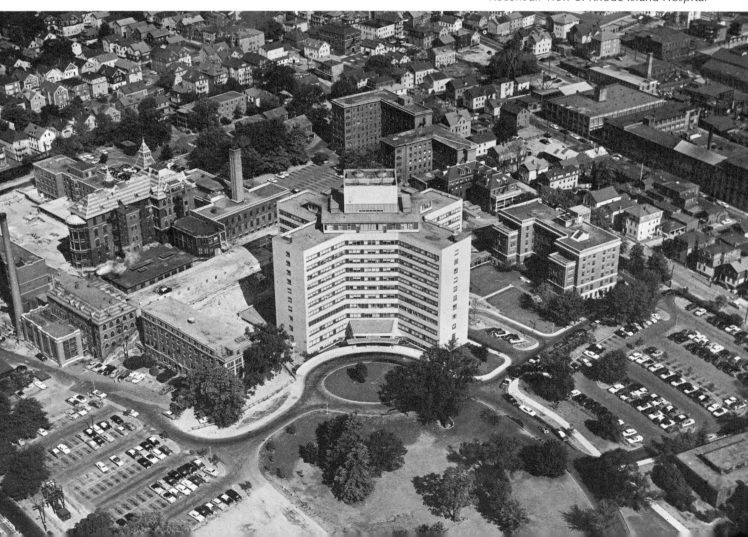

At the Head Office the Foreign Department became the International Department in the spring of 1962. It had expanded greatly due to the efforts of the Bank to identify with the world trade community and had become aggressive in stimulating foreign trade. It combed lists of Rhode Island manufacturers to determine whether a firm had a product to export, and tried to locate foreign firms interested in establishing branches in Rhode Island. It had become a clearing house for technical information, and, according to John M. Fraser, Jr., Vice President and Manager of the International Department in 1966, it became more service-oriented than any other department in the Trust Company, even concerning itself with nonbanking problems for customers. All the effort expended by this department was rewarded when the Presidential E for Export was given to Hospital Trust in 1963. That year the department had a 70 per cent gain in volume of transactions within one year and a 63 per cent gain in earnings the same year. The International Department continued its work with the federal government on community projects designed to increase the export potential of Rhode Island manufacturers and "continued to identify the name of the Trust Company with the international trading interests of the community." By 1966 the International Department, which had begun as a division of the Loan Department, had become a separate and distinct unit with only a slender tie remaining to the Loan Department. Close supervision, however, is given to all the other Loan Department divisions by E. Harris Howard III, Vice President and Senior Loan Officer, who succeeded William R. Innis to that position in 1963.

By the time the E for Export was awarded to the Bank, Clarence H. Gifford, Jr., was President. Born in Kentucky, he was a graduate of Peekskill Military Academy and Brown University, class of 1936. He had worked in the investment field and then joined the Phenix National Bank in 1948. He had been Vice President of the Phenix when it was absorbed by Hospital Trust and had come to the Trust Company as Vice President and Loan Officer. In 1962 he had been elected Executive Vice President and in 1963 assumed the duties of President. His first Annual Report contained many interesting facts. Business in 1963, he said, expanded as the Cuban crisis passed and confidence in President Johnson was demonstrated after President Kennedy's assassination in November, 1963. Mr. Gifford also pointed out that "techniques of servicing customers are always under review and change in an evolutionary manner from year to year." In a message to the staff of the Bank published in the house organ, *Around the Clock*, he said: "In this era of electronics, spacecraft and automation, let us not lose sight of the importance of the personal touch in our everyday lives here at the Bank. Remember, we have a tremendous asset to sell — the fine services of our bank — through You — a very integral part of the Hospital Trust's team. Customers are the life blood of this or any other organization. They deserve the most courteous and attentive treatment we can give them. Let's be sure Hospital Trust gives the best service in any area." To serve with Mr. Gifford, William R. Innis, the son of William S. Innis who served the Bank in this position from 1936 to 1943, was elected Executive Vice President. At the same time, C. Culver Towle was elected Secretary.

By 1964, the year President Johnson declared war on poverty, and the great civil rights battles were raging, the "blue ribbon service" theme had been developed for the Trust Company. Even the format of the Annual Report that year reflected the blue ribbon theme. In April Mr. Gifford began a round of visits to all the branches of the Rhode Island Hospital Trust Company for a series of "Coffee Hours with the President," the purpose of which was to convince people that "it is not the bricks and mortar that make Hospital Trust a bank, but the people who are in it."

On March 2, 1964, the former Wickford Savings Bank began business as a branch of Hospital Trust. In June the Auto Bank at the 'Gansett Shopping Center in East Providence opened and received a great deal of publicity. It was an experiment, opened for the convenience of customers who otherwise might have to drive in heavy traffic to other Hospital Trust banking offices. The Auto Bank emphasized efficiency, economy, and customer convenience. In its first year it served about fifty people an hour, 70 per cent of them in their cars.

In July, 1964, Mr. Gifford was one of 250 leading businessmen throughout the country to be invited to lunch at the White House for an exchange of views on the state of the nation with President Johnson.

In this same year the Savings Department was converted to computerized bookkeeping. (As the Trust Company would approach its one hundredth anniversary, the third generation of computers would be installed and the computer would have had an impact on almost every department.) By 1965 the electronic age reached further into the heart of the Bank with DepositPlate for checking account customers and $averPlate (passbook no longer necessary) for savings account customers. Also a billing program for the medical and dental professions, the Medac System, was launched. This resulted in the establishment of a new department — the Computer Services Division, created to sell the Bank's computer services to outside firms.

With the electronic age in full bloom, more and more people at the Trust Company were in contact with the public. This, William R. Innis, Executive Vice President in 1966, has said, is the way it should be: "A bank ought to be

Hurricane Barrier and Pumping Station

the personality of the people in it." He has pointed out that for generations the public has felt that bankers were cold and inhuman and that now that the staff of the Bank is released from running machines, it can do much to enhance the corporate image of the Trust Company in the eyes of the customers.

Going one step further, Mr. Gifford has stated that he feels that the officers of the Bank, the Board of Directors, and the personnel must take a stand on issues and to that end its officers and staff must be informed. On the eve of the centennial observance of the founding of Hospital Trust, Mr. Gifford would speak of a reaffirmation of the Bank's awareness of its responsibilities to the community. Mr. Gifford's own civic activities are extensive. He is trustee or director of sixteen charitable organizations, and in 1967 he will be general chairman of the United Fund. He is also a director of fourteen businesses and a corporate member of three hospitals. This feeling of responsibility comes down in a direct line from Mr. Binney, the first President, in whom the civic sense was so strong that "he found it a keen pleasure . . . to be able to render a signal service to the community."

138

Not only the spirit of community feeling goes back to Mr. Binney's day, but the names of many officers, Directors, and members of the staff remain the same. Sons, grandsons, nephews, and other descendants of the original corporators and of the men first connected with the Trust Company continue to serve the Company in the present day. The men in the Goddard family of Providence, for instance, have served as directors for a century, one generation succeeding the previous one to the position of Senior Director since 1867: Thomas Poynton Ives Goddard served from 1867 to 1874; Robert H. I. Goddard

Westminster Shoppers Mall — opened 1966

from 1874 to his death in 1916; Robert H. I. Goddard from 1908 to 1959; and currently R. H. I. Goddard, Jr., a member of the Board, has served since 1938. The Tafts, also, two generations of them, have been Directors from 1873 to 1942; the Sharpe family has served from 1896 to 1955; and the Metcalf family from 1900 to 1957. More than one generation of many other families, too, have served on the staff and as officers of the Trust Company.

By the end of 1965 Hospital Trust's net operating earnings were up 11.2 per cent over 1964. Its total assets were in excess of $475,000,000. The Annual Report for 1965 showed that all the figures had increased: total number of loans, 47,644; safe deposit rentals, 10,538; accounts (Checking, CheckMaster, Savings, etc.), 145,639; stockholders, 3,885; staff, 1,017. There were twenty-four branch banking locations and the Head Office. This was the first Annual Report incorporating certain changes in the method of presenting figures and Mr. Gifford explained these changes:

A year ago last August Congress enacted legislation which amended the Securities Exchange Act of 1934 to include banks with total assets of over $1 million and 750 or more stockholders among the companies subject to requirements of the Act. The Federal Reserve Board administers and enforces the new law for state-chartered banks that are members of the Federal Reserve System and has issued Regulation F to implement the provisions of this legislation. Compliance with Regulation F has necessitated the restatement of certain items in our reported figures of prior years.

Projected for 1966 were new facilities for some branches and additional space at the Head Office, mainly to supply larger and better quarters for all operating departments. E. Herbert Casperson, Vice President, is in charge of Operations, a department responsible for all operation procedures throughout the Trust Company and its branches.

In 1966 the Rhode Island Foundation celebrated its fiftieth anniversary. The financial management of the foundation had been turned over to the Rhode Island Hospital Trust Company in 1916. The income from it has been disbursed by order of a committee consisting of five members, all civic-minded leaders of the community. During the first half century there have been only three men in charge of the committee. The first was Ernest A. Harris, Trust Officer in charge of charitable trusts from 1920 to 1932. John H. Wells, Vice President of the Trust Company, served from 1932 to 1955, or almost two-thirds of the foundation's life. The current Executive Director is Robert W. Kenny.

Also, 1966 was the fortieth year the Trust Company had been administering the Avice Borda bequest of $50,000 left to "the Council of Narragansett Pier, Rhode Island, of the Boy Scouts of America, to be used under the supervision of the proper officials of that organization to aid the carrying on of its work and effecting its admirable purpose." Avice Borda was a member of the famous Sprague family — a daughter-in-law of the Civil War Governor of Rhode Island, William Sprague. The failure of the Sprague mills and banks in Rhode Island in 1873 had caused a financial depression in this state. When they failed, Zechariah Chafee, a member of the first Board of Directors of the Trust Company and President and Treasurer of Builders Iron Foundry, had been appointed sole trustee of all of the Sprague's property. With no experience in the textile field he had taken over the supervision of the mills under a trust mortgage. In 1966 the last of the Sprague mansions came on the market and was purchased by the Cranston Historical Society. The *Evening Bulletin* reported on May 11: "The society will borrow $70,000 from the Rhode Island Hospital Trust toward this." (The price of the house was $100,000.) In various ways the Bank has served this family, as it has many others, for almost a century.

As this history of the Bank's first one hundred years is being concluded, the nation's attention is directed to a "tight money situation." In addition to financing the Vietnam conflict and our so-called Great Society program, the demand for money has exceeded the supply. As an added burden, the federal government has not exercised fiscal restraints, leaving it to the Federal Reserve Board to attempt to combat inflation through fiscal controls.

The prime rate charged by Hospital Trust along with other banks in the country increased four times between December, 1965, and August, 1966. To obtain loanable funds, banks raised their savings interest little by little. At this writing, interest paid on savings deposits and the rate charged for loans are at an all-time high.

Near the close of its tenth decade the Trust Company was among the top fifty trust companies in America, the oldest trust company in New England, and one hundred and first (in 1965) among the large banks in the nation. It had withstood assaults by man and nature: financial panics, hurricanes, and tidal waves. It had grown with the times, always evolving new methods for accomplishing the same goal — to serve Rhode Islanders and Rhode Island. And with the changes it had for one hundred years adhered to the statement in its first advertisement: "This company is empowered by its charter to reserve money in trust or in deposit and to act as Administrator, Assignee or Receiver whether by appointment of court, or of individuals. It is also a chartered safe deposit company."

The Head Office of the Bank can be seen from great distances and towers over the pedestrian standing on the sidewalk; but this visible part, like

141

an iceberg, gives no indication of the massive structure invisible to the eye. That structure was built year after year, decade after decade, by the community-minded officers and board members of the Trust Company. At the Head Office and at the branches and facilities all over Rhode Island the staff of the Bank has participated actively in the life of Providence and this state. The Rhode Island Hospital Trust Company is now fixed in the life of the community and not only individuals but other institutions as well look to it for guidance and advice. Many depend on it; but it, in turn, depends on many and this interdependence is what makes it so much a part of the life of the area. With the help of the residents of Rhode Island it will continue to grow and to serve the state in the coming century as it has in the past one hundred years.

FORWARD IN TIME

The strictly formal atmosphere that once prevailed in the Trust Company no longer exists. The President meets his customers over coffee, the tellers quip with the depositors, blue carnations to signify friendly service are handed out by pretty girls, officers drive bulldozers to break ground for new buildings, and a bottle of champagne is broken to open a new branch. All kinds of informal happenings take place, but a certain sense of order prevails, for, after all, banking is a serious business.

What methods will be used to conduct this business in the future? Such drastic changes have occurred in banking in the last half century that it is difficult to imagine what other changes remain for the next fifty years. No matter how many changes will occur, there will be one constant: the Trust Company's responsibility to the community. The idiom may be different from the language used by the incorporators, the men may be different and the methods, but that will remain. For the rest . . . Patrick Henry is quoted as having said, "I have but one lamp by which my feet are guided and that is the lamp of experience. I know of no way of judging of the future but by the past."

The Rhode Island Hospital Trust Company, on its record of growth and dedicated service to the community from 1867 to 1967, stands ready to be judged and, therefore, enters its second century with confidence.

BANK STAFF

January 1, 1967 — Listed Alphabetically

Abrams, Hope S.
Adams, George M.
Ahmuty, Olive L.
Aldrich, Donald J.
Alexander, Herbert R., Jr.
Alker, Dorothy M.
Allen, Helen P.
Allen, Pamela B.
Allen, Roselyn B.
Altruda, Cathleen R.
Amaral, Joyce E.
Ambrosino, Frank F., Jr.
Ames, Ruth B.
Anderson, Alden M.
Andrade, Janice E.
Andreozzi, Janice R.
Andrews, Sydney J.
Angell, Mildred
Annis, Roderick J.
Anzevino, Judith C.
Araujo, Joseph
Archambault, Barbara A.
Areson, Raymond F.
Armstrong, Mary I.
Arnold, Edith M.
Arnold, Linda J.
Artesani, Joyce E.
Atkinson, Frederick E.
Auclair, Priscilla A.
Audette, Alice R.
Augusta, Charles T.
Axile, Manuel R., Jr.

Bacon, Helen L.
Bain, Thomas M.
Baldwin, Robert H.
Barden, Melbourne R.
Barker, Bertha
Barker, Chester N.
Barkett, Joseph J., Jr.
Barr, Donald W.
Barrett, George E.
Barrett, William F., Jr.
Barsamian, Clara
Bates, Robert A.
Bauer, Eunice C.
Baxter, Robert B.
Bayha, Cynthia A.
Beal, Arthur W.

Beard, Betty Ann
Beattie, George L.
Beaubien, Brenda J.
Beauchemin, Armand
Beaudet, Arthur J.
Beaulieu, Helen F.
Beaumont, Barbara A.
Beaumont, Bertrand A.
Bejma, Fred B.
Beliveau, Charlene A.
Belknap, Claude L.
Bell, Judith S.
Bennett, Chester C.
Bennett, Lloyd E.
Bennett, Malcolm W.
Benson, Richard W.
Berard, Jeannette B.
Berghorn, Jane L.
Bergquist, Edith M.
Berkery, Vincent D.
Berube, Armand N.
Bianco, Joseph P.
Bigelow, Helen W.
Bigney, Brian L.
Bilida, Bernice J.
Bingemann, Pamela W.
Blackinton, Carol M.
Blair, Harold D.
Blake, Virginia D.
Blaydes, Clarence H., Jr.
Bobola, Catherine T.
Bockes, Robert A.
Boden, Herbert H., Jr.
Boffi, Jeanne A.
Bonaccorsi, Elaine P.
Boorom, Sharon J.
Borek, John C.
Borge, Dulce
Borges, Roberta J.
Boss, Hazel M.
Botelho, Patricia A.
Bouchard, Paul A.
Bourne, Merilynn C.
Bowering, Richard E.
Bowser, Nancy S.
Boyle, Thomas W.
Brandao, Irene A.
Brassard, Lucille J.
Brayman, George E.

Brennan, Robert K.
Brett, Susan L.
Brett, Warren G.
Bridge, Marion B.
Briggs, George W.
Briggs, M. Loretta
Briggs, Robert M.
Brillon, Joan L.
Brillon, Mary E.
Brindamour, Beatrice F.
Bromiley, Albert
Brook, Thomas E.
Brousseau, Mary J.
Brown, Frank R. H.
Brown, Glenn C.
Brown, Irma R.
Brown, Stephen M.
Buck, John D.
Buonaiuto, Teresa S.
Burbank, Waldo H.
Burke, Judith E.
Burke, Marian E.
Burlingame, Janet R.
Burns, John M.
Burns, Joyce T.
Busby, Adeline L.
Bushey, Barbara L.
Butler, Ruth E.
Byrnes, Robert E.

Caine, Linda M.
Calamar, Kathleen E.
Caldwell, Gloria J.
Caldwell, Gretchen D.
Cambio, Elaine A.

Auto Bank, East Providence

Cambio, Enis L.
Campbell, James R.
Canning, Barbara B.
Capuano, Leonard D.
Capwell, Marjorie
Carey, William C.
Carleton, Virginia
Carlisle, Anna T.
Carlson, Dolores L.
Carney, Francis G.
Carpenter, George J.
Carter, Elaine M.
Cartwright, Lois B.
Casey, Paul E., Jr.
Casperson, E. Herbert
Cate, Frances E.
Caverly, Deborah A.
Ceselski, Judith D.
Champoux, Phyllis
Chapman, Ellen F.
Chapman, Richard P., Jr.
Charpentier, Alice B.
Chartier, Shirley A.
Chase, Nancy C.
Chiarillo, Joanne M.
Chorney, Robert D.
Christy, Theresa L.
Ciba, Casimir M.
Cicchetti, Patricia A.
Clark, Richard P.
Codman, Daniel S.
Colangelo, Christine
Colavecchio, Angela M.
Coletti, Donald B.
Colvin, Alice K.

Colvin, Theodore D.
Colwell, George E.
Comire, Richard A.
Conaty, Anne E.
Conley, Eleanor L.
Conley, Elizabeth E.
Connery, Marjorie A.
Connolly, Barbara E.
Connolly, Mary E.
Connolly, Robert G.
Connors, Charles W., Jr.
Constantineau, Laurette M.
Conte, Virginia S.
Corcoran, Velma L.
Cordeiro, Dennis A.
Corder, Patricia K.
Cormier, John A.
Cornelius, Charles B.
Corvese, Ernest, Jr.
Costello, Robert
Cotnoir, James R.
Cotoia, Jean M.
Cotter, Margaret W.
Cotton, Mary Lou
Cottrell, Robert A.
Couper, Frances A.
Cousineau, Madeleine R.
Coyne, Catherine M.
Creaney, Robert C.
Crepeau, E. Elaine
Croasdale, Judith A.
Croft, Dianna M.
Cross, Earl F.
Crowley, John E.
Cull, Susan J.
Cummings, George W.
Cunningham, Marilyn J.
Cunningham, Patrick J.
Curran, Leonard J.
Currier, Albert A.
Currier, Mary L. T.
Curt, David A.
Curvelo, Charles J.
Cybulski, Stanley P.

Dailey, Mary R.
D'Ambra, Antonetta J.
Dana, Severyn S.
Daniels, John L.

Danielson, Kenneth S.
Darcy, Karen A.
Darling, Althea L.
Davidson, Emily E.
Davie, Bruce D.
Dawley, Frances K.
Dean, James F.
Dean, Sharon E.
DeCorte, Patricia A.
DeFalco, Henry D.
DeLemos, Robert L.
Delicio, Ella J.
Delisle, Julien J.
DelNero, M. L. Preece
DeLuca, Jean M.
Demers, Omer C.
DeNicola, Vera C.
Desautel, Gloria J.
Desmarais, Celine
DesRoches, Ruth E.
Devoe, Richard W.
DiDonato, Germano
DiMaio, Sandra P.
DiNuccio, Donna M.
DiPonte, Judith M.
Dixon, Delroy L.
Doctor, Mabel
Domina, E. Curtis
Donovan, Robert L.
DosReis, Albertina M.
Downie, Esther J.
Downing, Everett J., Jr.
Drolet, Suzanne
Drury, James J.
Dube, Florence D.
Duhamel, Eleanore M.
Dupuis, Diane D.
Durling, Lee R.

Eannarino, Edward R.
Ebert, Ernest W., III
Edds, Carol
Edward, Andrea M.
Egan, Lawrence J., Jr.
Ehnes, Helen J.
Eknoian, Sarah
Ellinwood, Edwin E.
Ellinwood, George W.
Ellis, John H.

Howard Building Office, Providence

Elsner, Helga
Emmel, Joanne M.
Ennis, Hazel E.
Erickson, Beverly J.
Erickson, Carolyn E.
Evans, Warren O., Jr.
Everett, Sylvia

Fagan, Arthur W.
Fagan, Eleanor G.
Famiglietti, Anthony, Jr.
Feeney, Thomas L.
Ferreira, Eugene A.
Ferrell, Vioris N.
Fiddes, Donna J.
Fiddes, George R.
Field, Harold J.
Figueiredo, Richard
Finerty, John F.
Fiore, Joseph C.
Fischer, Therese A.
Fisher, Linda L.
Fitts, Clark D.
Flamand, Paul E.
Flynn, Charles F.
Flynn, Donald W.
Flynn, Raymond J.
Flynn, Thomas F., Jr.
Fogarty, Marion E.
Forget, Marguerite B.
Forrest, Robert H.
Forte, Dora M.
Fortin, Louise A.
Fox, Russell S.
Frain, Anthony J.
Franceschi, Maria
Fraser, John M., Jr.
Frattarelli, Louise M.
French, Doris I.
Frost, Herbert H.
Furber, Carol A.

Gage, Willard H., Jr.
Gaiga, Angela C.
Gaines, Sandra A.
Gardiner, Raymond W.
Gardner, Rachel E.
Gartner, George C., Jr.
Gaudreau, Conrad E.

Gaudreau, Dorothy T.
Gavin, Anne R.
Gemma, Elizabeth
Gendreau, Theresa M.
Gentes, Edmond E.
Geoffroy, Margaret M.
George, Anthony J.
Gerrior, Jeanne E.
Giampietro, Joan M.
Giangrande, Patricia A.
Gibbs, Robert C.
Giblin, Anne M.
Gifford, Clarence H., Jr.
Giles, Charles S., Jr.
Gilkenson, Albert H.
Gill, Matthew J.
Gilmore, C. Henry, Jr.
Gimber, Karen L.
Gladhill, Joan M.
Gleadow, Charles E., Jr.
Glover, William J.
Glynn, Katherine E.
Godbout, James J.
Godfrey, Richard D.
Godin, Russell F.
Goff, Carol A.
Goff, Marlene A.
Gomberg, Frances
Grable, Dorothy F.
Grady, Carol A.
Grady, Raymond J.
Gray, J. Russell
Grayson, Betty
Greenlund, Svea B.
Gregoire, Raymond J.
Gregory, Leslie C.
Grocer, Gertrude M.
Groeneveld, Agnes B.
Grosch, Edna M.
Gross, Charles E.
Guay, Janice E.
Guercia, Virgillo E.
Guillette, Norman H.
Guiot, Joseph
Gushee, Judith A.

Hackett, Eleanor L.
Haganey, Francis J., Jr.
Haigh, Jack

Hall, Marjorie A.
Handy, Judith L.
Haracz, Linda L.
Hardy, Ruth S.
Harris, Townes M., Jr.
Hartigan, Dorothy A.
Hassell, Frank A.
Hastie, Janice E.
Hastings, Claudia J.
Hathaway, Anne S.
Heap, Elizabeth H.
Heaton, Alan J.
Hein, Doris I.
Hemmings, Ronald C.
Henn, Helen M.
Henry, Robert R.
Henthorne, Granville V.
Hewey, Martha E.
Higginbotham, Lois J.
Hines, Arthur M.
Hirsch, Helen P.
Hladyk, Mary Anne
Hodder, Louise E.
Hodges, Mary Jane
Hogle, Bette A.
Hohlmaier, Ronald E.
Hoisington, Helen B.
Holcomb, Lillian H.
Holloway, Judith A.
Holmes, Martha B.
Holmes, Richard L.
Holst, Barbara W.
Holt, Kathleen
Honiball, Richard D. D.
Hooks, Donald S.

147

Johnston, John G., Jr.
Jordan, Sylvia S.
Juber, Marilyn
Juskalian, Barbara J.

Kalunian, Joanne R.
Kanelakos, Peter J.
Kane, John P., Jr.
Kavanaugh, Shirley A.
Kearney, Joseph P.
Keeler, Anna M.
Keenan, Robert F.
Kelly, Mortimer T.
Kennedy, Eugene J.
Kennelly, Anna A.
Kent, Clifford C.
Kerr, Anna E.
Kilburn, K. Wilson
Killabian, Agnes
King, Evelyn M.
King, Linda G.
Knight, Donald K.
Knowles, Lawrence G., Jr.
Korkosz, Rita L.
Krantz, Rosemary

La Bella, Dominick R.
Laliberte, Irene K.
Lamoureux, Oscar L.
Lane, Howard D.
Langelia, Carol A.
Langhorn, Joseph
Lanoue, Barbara M.
Lapointe, Robert J.
Lareau, Douglas S.
Larence, Yvette A.
Larson, Janice
LaSalandra, Catherine A.
Lavallee, Linda M.
Lavimodiere, J. P.
Lawlor, Ruth M.
Lawrence, Lynn W.
Lawrence, Steven C.
Laycock, Bruce A.
Leander, Evelyn M.
Leary, Patricia A.
Leary, William A.
LeBeau, Arthur F.
Lebeuf, Edmond L.

LeBlanc, Eugenia G.
LeBlanc, Maurice H.
LeBlanc, Robert W.
Lee, Henry R.
Legare, Donat A.
Leja, Frances A.
Lemieux, Joanna H.
Lemmens, Judith A.
L'Etoile, Claire E.
Levein, Ruth
Lewis, Barbara E.
Lial, Maryann
Lincourt, Joan E.
Linehan, Lucy P.
Lippka, Ray E.
Lipscomb, Patricia L.
Little, Raymond B.
Little, Stevan B.
Loftus, Nancy E.
Loomis, Richard S.
Lorange, George M.
Lord, Richard H.
Lozier, Fordyce R.
Lucas, Mary E.
Luther, Lucille I.

Macaulay, Murray K.
MacDonald, Margaret V.
MacQueen, John, Jr.
Maddern, Edward B.
Maddren, Donna M.
Mahoney, Audrey E.
Mainelli, Patricia A.
Major, Nathaniel
Makepeace, Charles R., Jr.
Malito, Frank F.
Malley, Arthur W.
Malley, Gail E.
Malouin, Philip A.
Mancini, Carolyn A.
Manion, Matthew J.
Manning, Bernice
Mansolillo, Evelyn V.
Marble, Eleanor A.
Marciano, Cynthia R.
Marcotte, Robert J.
Mariscal, Carlos I.
Marshall, U. Jean
Martel, Patricia D.

Hopkins, Cheryl J.
Horton, Richard T.
Hosbond, Martin R.
Houlton, Marcia L.
Howard, E. Harris, III
Howe, John Timothy
Hudson, Kathleen M.
Hufnagel, J. Earl
Hustedt, Charles E.
Hutton, Barbara M.
Hyatt, Karen
Hynes, William H.

Iacone, Nellie
Iannoli, Ruby D.
Iasimone, James A.
Inman, Alfred C.
Innis, William R.
Irons, Ardell J.
Iselin, Archer
Izzo, Michael R.

Jackson, Lewis B.
Jacoy, Arthur W.
Jalette, Germaine C.
James, Helen C.
Jayne, Catherine I.
Jeffery, Clara E.
Jeffrey, Donald J.
Jehan, Norman P.
Johnson, Charlotte E.
Johnson, Janice
Johnson, Judith A.
Johnson, Katherine E.
Johnson, Nora

148

Martin, Dorothy E.
Martin, Edward A.
Martin, Joan A.
Martin, Michelle M.
Martin, Roy F.
Martin, Ruth E.
Martone, Louise D.
Mason, Curtis W.
Mason, Dorothy A.
Mason, Robert C.
Massaro, Thomas
Massoyan, Juliette S.
Maston, Bolac J.
Mattera, Sylvia
Mattia, Helen A.
Mauran, Duncan H.
McAndrews, Olive
McAskill, J. Norman, Jr.
McAuslan, Frederic T.
McCabe, Margaret F.
McCaffrey, Betty F.
McCaffrey, James J.
McCarthy, Kevin P.
McCaughey, H. Francis
McCaughey, William D., Jr.
McCombs, Donna A.
McCoy, Doris M.
McCraw, William H.
McDermott, Ann P.
McDonald, Alice C.
McGowan, Eileen
McGowan, Marguerite L.
McGrane, Mary D.
McGregor, Donald F.
McGuire, G. Elaine
McHugh, Maureen A.
McKenna, Martina E.
McLachlan, William
McLellan, Mildred L.
McMahon, Dorothy L.
McMahon, Felicia J.
McManus, Alice T.
McNeilis, Lois C.
McStay, Richard A.
Mello, Robert Joseph
Melone, Kathleen P.
Menard, Claire M.
Mercier, Charles J.
Meservey, Lewis C.

Meservey, Muriel E.
Metcalf, Houghton P., Jr.
Mikula, Helen
Miles, T. Arthur
Miller, Claire M.
Miranda, Joseph R.
Miranda, Virginia M.
Mischler, Beatrice R.
Misiaszek, Matthew J.
Moody, Carol A.
Moody, Marcella W.
Mooney, James A.
Moralee, Edith L.
Morin, Gail S.
Moulton, Laura A.
Mowbray, Sarah A.
Mowry, Helen L.
Mozzetta, Anita
Mucci, Bethany J.
Mulhall, Alfred J.
Munro, Eleanor T.
Murphy, Donald D.
Murphy, Dorothy M.
Murphy, John F.
Murphy, John F., III
Murphy, Lawrence R.
Murphy, Teresa M.
Myers, Marjorie D.

Nachbar, Florence J.
Neale, Gordon T.
Nekrewicz, Andrea A.
Nelle, James T.
Nelson, Albert R.
Nelson, John W., III
Nelson, Wilbur
Newbauer, Miriam F.
Newcomb, Virginia L.
Newman, Raymond V.
Nichols, Chester R., Jr.
Nolan, Eileen A.
Norberg, Gladys H.
Nordquist, Phillip E.
Nulman, Charlotte G.
Nyberg, Donald E.

O'Brien, Catherine A.
O'Brien, Fred E., Jr.
O'Brien, Nancy J.

O'Brien, William E.
O'Connell, John A., Jr.
O'Donahue, Margaret A.
Ogilvie, George M., Jr.
Ogni, John M.
Olivier, Diane L.
Olson, Doris C.
Orabone, Richard J.
O'Riley, Madeline
O'Rourke, Thomas J.
Orsini, Samuel R.
Ottaviano, Gerard H., Jr.
Ouellette, Lorraine L.
Ouimette, Linda L.
Ouloosian, Betty

Paglia, Catherine R.
Palmieri, Rosalie M.
Panzarella, Mary A.
Paolino, Sylvia
Paolozzi, Paula Rae
Paquet, Carol A.
Paquet, Donald
Paquette, Judith A.
Paquin, Angela S.
Paquin, Susan
Paradis, Leo J.
Paradis, Nelson J.
Parker, Gordon L., Jr.
Parker, Meredith A.
Parkin, Agnes H.
Parks, Dorothy M.
Pattison, Corinne A.
Paulson, George A.
Paye, Carter B.

Dexter Street Office, Pawtucket

Pearson, Roy I. L.
Peirce, Thomas J.
Pelkey, Preston T.
Pelopida, Ruth E.
Pennell, James E.
Penta, Amelia
Pereira, Eileen C.
Perry, John F.
Perry, Sandra A.
Pesaturo, Arthur A., Jr.
Pesula, John M.
Petersen, Helen K.
Peterson, Bertha E.
Peterson, N. Eric
Pezzi, Jacqueline M.
Pfeiffer, Barbara A.
Phillips, Elizabeth A.
Phillips, Lynn R.
Piccirillo, Maureen A.
Pierce, Sally M.
Pierson, Hazel E. L.
Pigeon, Karen L.
Pina, Lawrence A.
Pinson, Martin T.
Place, Charles C.
Poisson, Louise L.
Poole, Barbara W.
Potter, Adelia M.
Potter, Gloria M.
Potter, L. Irene
Prata, Mary M.
Pratt, Harold D.
Price, Barbara C.
Price, Hilda H.
Provost, Maurice N.

Quam, Mary
Queenan, Edward M.
Quinham, Elizabeth M.
Quinn, Brenda M.

Radway, Robert W.
Rainey, Richard N., Jr.
Raleigh, Susan
Randall, Harold W.
Randall, Peter R.
Randlett, Jennie F.
Raso, Assunta
Raymond, Gertrude L.
Raymond, Jeannette
Raymond, Lina E.
Read, H. Milton, Jr.
Read, Meredyth F.
Reagan, LeRoy S., Jr.
Reedenauer, Kathleen M.
Reels, Floyd T.
Reynolds, Alfred S.
Reynolds, Cynthia E.
Reynolds, Eleanor C.
Reynolds, R. Foster, 3rd
Rhee, Michael J.
Rhine, Thomas M.
Richard, Jeanne L.
Richard, Robert E.
Rinaldi, Daniel A.
Rioles, Christine F.
Riordan, Rosamond C.
Roberts, Eleanor L.
Roberts, William R.
Robidoux, Ronald R.
Robinson, Etta M.
Roche, Mary T.
Rodinsky, Beverly A.
Rondeau, Normand D.
Rooney, Jacqueline A.
Rose, Raymond F.
Ross, Evelyn S.
Ross, James E.
Ross, Murray N.
Rousseau, Louise K.
Rousseau, Rita L.
Rousselle, Madeleine E.
Rowan, Bernice E.
Rowles, C. Gordon, Jr.
Rubin, Carol E.

Ruest, Maurice F.
Russell, Edgar F., Jr.
Ryan, Helen F.
Rylands, Suzanne

Sabin, Donald W.
Sagan, Florence M.
Sample, Sarah M.
Santillo, Janice A.
Savastano, John
Savoie, Xavier
Scotti, Nino D. B.
Scotti, Rosemarie
Seamans, Elizabeth
Seward, Christine E.
Shaffer, George K.
Shatzer, Elinor R.
Shaw, Margaret M.
Shepard, Nancy E.
Shepard, Noreen A.
Sherman, Winifred A.
Sherry, Gladys A.
Shore, Frances
Sickinger, Carolyn M.
Silva, Dolores A.
Simmons, Louis K., Jr.
Simms, Albert H., Jr.
Simonds, Philip B.
Sinclair, Marjorie M.
Sjogren, Donald E.
Skober, John, Jr.
Slater, Robert D.
Sliney, Margaret E.
Smith, Carolyn L.
Smith, Francis S.
Smith, Jacqueline E.
Smith, Jessie H.
Smith, John J.
Smith, Kenneth P.
Smith, Paul D.
Smith, William F.
Smolan, Frances M.
Smyth, Stanley A.
Soares, John J., Jr.
Soares, Rosemary A.
Soucy, Linda N.
Sousa, Maria
Spingler, Mary A.
Spoerer, Henry G.

Wakefield Office

Edgewood Office, Cranston

Spreen, Kenneth R.
Spremulli, Anthony
Squire, Polly R.
Sroka, Christine
Stacy, Shirley T.
Statkiewicz, Ronald L.
Stawarz, Stanley J.
Stevens, Dorothy N.
Stewart, George E.
Stewart, James G.
Strahm, Janice B.
Straight, Robert E.
Strong, Howard R.
Stubbs, Virginia E.
Suffoletto, Sylvia
Sullivan, Elizabeth
Sullivan, Julia F.
Surkont, Roberta A.
Susi, Norma D.
Sweetland, Joan T.

Taft, Edward C.
Taft, Margaret A.
Tait, Adelaide E.
Tallman, Janet L.
Tallman, Raymond C.
Tattersall, Eileen M.
Tavares, Mary D.
Taylor, Donald H.
Taylor, Donald T., Jr.
Taylor, Ralph H.
Tebbetts, Ruth M.
Teixeira, Everett R.
Tessier, Judith C.
Tetrault, Doris M.
Tetreault, Claire Y.
Tetu, Suzanne M.
Thalmann, Mary E.
Theberge, Edward J.
Therrien, Diane M.
Thomas, Harold W.
Thompson, David L.
Thompson, Lynn C.
Thompson, Melissa E.
Thomson, William
Thornlimb, Ida M.
Thornlimb, Lois E.
Thumith, Aileen K.
Thurrott, Stephen F.

Tillinghast, Barbara H.
Tingle, Robert J.
Tingley, S. Bradford
Toolin, Kathleen M.
Toulmin, Peter N.
Tourigny, Karen A.
Tourony, Barbara E.
Towle, C. Culver
Tracy, Pauline B.
Treml, Joyce A.
Treworgy, Donna R.
Tullie, Judith J.
Turbitt, Robert A.
Tyks, Gladys H.
Tyrell, Carol A.
Tyrrell, Anne M.

Udall, Ralph O.
Ulbin, Mary M.
Ursillo, Albert G.

Vaill, Barry C.
Vallone, Marion M.
Vanasse, Gabrielle E.
Van Buren, Wyeth
Van Liew, Alfred B., II
Vanni, Elaiñe
Varden, George A.
Vendetti, Phyllis F.
Venditti, Palma
Vincenzo, Geraldine M.
Vose, Nathaniel M., Jr.

Walaska, Henry J.
Walker, Edward G., Jr.
Walker, Roy C.
Wall, John W.
Walsh, Marc J.
Waring, Marie C.
Watson, Sandra A.
Watterson, Richard H.
Waugh, Dorothy S.
Webster, Joan R.
Wells, Herbert C., Jr.
Welt, Marjorie
Wescott, Marcia N.
Westberg, Alice I.
Whipple, William D.
Whitaker, Howard B.

White, William W.
Whitney, Carol J.
Whittaker, Mildred
Whittaker, Paul H.
Whitworth, Ethel E.
Wigington, Andrew J.
Wilder, Barbara J.
Wiley, Victoria B.
Williams, John H.
Willis, Mary M.
Wilson, Dorothy M.
Wilson, William M.
Winsor, George W.
Wiseman, Marie A.
Wolfe, Patrick J.
Woodbridge, Henry S., Jr.
Woodmansee, William A.
Woolley, James F.
Wright, Arthur F.
Wright, Carol L.
Wright, Cynthia M.
Wynne, Clinton H.

Xavier, Barbara A.

Young, Frank, Jr.

Zambuco, Pasqualina T.
Ziobrowski, Mary Louise
Zuercher, Dorothea L.
Zurowski, Virginia M.

BUILDINGS' STAFF

January 1, 1967 — Listed Alphabetically

Anna Anderson
Clarence A. Anderson
Tessie L. Antos
Joan Augusta
Dorothea M. Auliff

Maria Barbosa
Mary Barboza
Edward Bardsley
Earnest M. Barnes
Amelia Bart
Lucien A. Bastien
Gozale Bedrosian
Maria Bettencourt
Herbert H. Boden, Jr.
Helen K. Bogdan
Gedeon A. Boisvert
Manuel Borges
Arminda Botelho
Maria Botelho
Mildred D. Boyd
Henry C. Breard
Mykola Buratczuk

Manuel Cabral
Maria H. Cabral
Angelo Calandra
Dorothy A. Carnegis
Walter Carter
Margaret A. Cavanaugh
Agnes Chakoian
Federico Ciampanelli, Jr.
Lillian Coey
Antonio Coimbra
Margaret M. Conway
Charles F. Corbett
Arthur Corrente
Francisca S. Costa
Margaret Costa
Maria D. Costa
Albert S. Cote
Aram E. Cote
John A. Cowell
Henry Crossman
Anna S. Cunningham

Howard G. Davis
Richard J. Dearnley
Hubert Deignan

Angel Derderian
Giragos DerManuelian
Emily C. DeSilva
Ernest J. Desjardins
Thelma Dias
Mary Docca
Rosalina Doro
Paul G. Dwyer

Agnes Eknoian

Anna Filanowff
Margaret A. Fitzpatrick
Giteria Fonseca
Maria D. Franco

Stefi Garisonas
Bernice C. Garrity
Theresa Gavrillen
Arthur Gengo
Natalizo Gervelis
Mary S. Gomes
Marie D. Gonsalo

Laurence A. Hadfield
Kenneth H. Hall
Jeremiah Harrington
Arthur I. Henault
Sarah Hercov
Geoffrey Hill
Johanna A. Hull
Douglas F. Huntley

Axel M. Johanson
Gustaf A. Johnson
John G. Johnston

Veneta Kanelakos
Agnes R. Kearns
Elaine G. Keegan
William J. Kiernan
Stanley Kogut
Zose Kriauciuniene

John Laba
Anna Lackey
Oliver J. Lafleur
Norman J. Landry
Gelassee Lavimodiere, Jr.

Edward S. Leamy
Oscar N. Lefebvre
Alfred Ledoux
Clarence R. Lewis

Antonetta McCaughey
James R. McLaughlin
Peter McNamee
Anna T. McSoley
Antonia C. Marcononis
David F. Mariani
Donald R. Martin
Sandra J. Masciarelli
Rose Mederios
Liduina Mederios
Mary Mederios
Sarsh Menissian
Howard J. Mersereau
Catherine Miller
William J. Monigan
Louise O. Morrison
Mary C. Morrissey
Francis A. Moulton
William E. Mullin

Frank Nakopinski

Thomas O'Gara
Alice Ogassian
Donald V. Olson
John T. O'Malley
Gerard A. Ouimet

Maria P. Pacheco
Minnie Papleuskas
Ernest R. Paquin
Emilia Perreira
Henry A. Perron
Mary Phillips
Chiara Piccirilli
Michael Pomoranski
Frieda A. Pueschel

Gladys Quigley
Nora S. Quigley

Rose Rahanian
Peter A. Reilly
Valerie Richard

152

Lillian L. Rickey
George W. Rose
Frank Ross, Jr.
Everett B. Rounds

Josephine Salema
Angelina Saudade
Joseph T. Schiboni
Vartig Shiranian
Anna Silva
Jesunia S. Silva
Maria F. Silva
Mary D. Silva
Rose T. Silva

Isobel Simas
Quentin T. Smith
William H. Smith
Ana M. Sousa
Mary Sousa
Harry P. Starkey
Sartenig S. Stepanian
John Stewart
Henry A. Stone
Petrone Sukys

Ann M. Tattersall
Maria N. Tavares
J. Frank Timperley

Leo J. Tondreau
Raymond A. Tondreau
Helen M. Toomey

Altoon Vanoian
Joseph T. Vensky
Fardina J. Vermette
Lillian Vigneau

Mary Wallin
Mildred A. Ware
Anne E. Wood

Thomas Young

*   *   *   *   *

ACKNOWLEDGMENTS

This book could not have been written without the help of everyone at the Rhode Island Hospital Trust Company who made the records of that institution available to me without reservation and who, in addition, granted interviews and set aside time for conferences in which they answered countless questions. I am indebted to them all.

I would also like to express my appreciation to the capable staff of the Reference Room at the Providence Public Library and the staff of the Rhode Island Historical Society who were tireless in their assistance. The State Library and the Archives proved to be other sources of valuable information.

My most sincere thanks to Grant Dugdale, Director of the Brown University Press, and to Anne Joseph for her editorial assistance.

Finally, I would like to thank my husband for his patience while I slowly worked my way out from under mounds of index cards and for his help with the manuscript in many ways.

Florence Parker Simister

We are indebted to the many organizations and individuals who have so graciously made available not only the many rare and interesting photographs included in this volume but many more for which space could not be found.

Permission to reproduce those pictures shown has been given by the following:

Adler Art Associates
Brown University
Department of Public Works, State of R.I.
Greater Providence Chamber of Commerce
Providence College News Bureau
Providence Journal Library
Providence Public Library
The Providence Visitor
Rhode Island Development Council
The Rhode Island Historical Society
Title Guarantee Company of R.I.
U.S. Naval Air Station, Quonset Point, R.I.
Alfred J. Viera